HISTORY OF THE WORLD

Ancient Greece and Rome

CHERRYTREE BOOKS

A Cherrytree Book

This edition adapted by
A S Publishing

First published by Editoriale Jaca Book s.p.a. Milan
© Editoriale Jaca 1992
First English edition published in United States
by Raintree Publishers
English translation © Raintree Publishers Limited Partnership
Translation by Hess-Inglin Translation Service

This edition first published 1992
by Cherrytree Press Ltd
a subsidiary of
The Chivers Company Ltd
Windsor Bridge Road
Bath, Avon BA2 3AX

Copyright © Cherrytree Press Ltd 1992

British Library Cataloguing in Publication Data
    Ancient Greece and Rome. – (History of the world)
    I. Williams, Brian II. Series
    937

    ISBN 0-7451-5161-2

Printed in Hong Kong by Imago Publishing Ltd

CONTENTS

Pelagonia

MACEDONIA

Abdera

MT. OLYMPUS

LEMNOS

EPIRUS

Dodona

THESSALY

CORCYRA

AETOLIA

Thermopylae

PHOCIS

LOCRIS

Delphi

EUBOEA

Chalcis

Eretria

BOEOTIA

Thebes

ITHACA

CEPHALLENIA

ATTICA

ACHAEA

Megara

ZACYNTHUS

Corinth

SALAMINA

Athens

Piraeus

Olympia

Mycenae

Argos

ARGOLIS

Aegina

Tiryns

Epidaurus

Calauria

MESSENIA

Sparte

Pylos

LACONICA

Delos

AEGEAN SEA

MEDITERRANEAN SEA

Cydonia

Knossos

Gortina

CRETE

Phaestu

THE WORLD OF THE GREEKS

Minoan and Mycenaean towns (civilization of the palaces) 2000-1250 B.C.

Towns and city-states (archaic and classical Greek civilization) 800-350 B.C.

ASIA MINOR

Centres of cults, feasts and games

Principal areas of expansion of the Dorians between 1200 and 800 B.C.

Expansion of the Ionians between 1200 and 800 B.C.

Expansion of the Aeolians between 1200 and 800 B.C.

Ancient Greek peoples

SAMOTHRACE

Propontis

Byzantium

Troy

AEOLIS

Mytilene

LESBOS

Phocaea

Chios

IONIA

CHIOS

Ephesus

SAMOS

Samos

Priene

Miletus

CARIA

Halicarnassus

THERA

Thera

DORIS

Rhodes

RHODES

PAMPHYLIA

Gournia

GREEK CIVILIZATION

In the eighth century B.C., one of the most important chapters of human history was about to open. The group of islands and peninsulas which today is known as Greece was to be the stage for extraordinary events.

Highly developed civilizations had flourished even earlier both in Greece and on the large island of Crete. The Greek towns of Mycenae and Tiryns flourished, and hosted a great blossoming of the arts around 1400-1200 B.C. This period is called the Mycenaean period. It was followed by the so-called Dark Ages between 1200 and 800 B.C. Mycenaean civilization, which was ruled by powerful lords who lived in large palaces, was destroyed by drought, raids, and a progressive decay of the Greek towns. During this time of decline, the previous period began to be looked on as a heroic and mythical age.

Politics

The art of politics was born in Greece. The polis, or city-state, was a genuine Greek achievement. Noble citizens, at first, and then an increasingly large number of ordinary citizens were involved in politics. The Greek people conceived a system of written laws that stated the rights of the powerful as well as those of any other citizen. Everyone had to obey the written laws. This system of laws was proof of the political intellect of the Greek people. They did not trust the judgement of a sovereign (a supreme ruler) with power to decide what was right and wrong. In difficult times or because of internal clashes, the Greeks often resorted to putting the rule of the polis in the hands of tyrants. In spite of this, their love for law and justice was never totally obscured.

Philosophy

A major philosophical movement originated in Greece. At its core was the importance of reason, considered the ultimate characteristic of humans. Greek rationality was to become a reference point for all Western civilization. However, Greek thought was often tinged with pessimism. Greek philosophers considered humans incapable of finding the answers to the deepest questions and of understanding the mystery of death.

Art

A great appreciation for the beauty, intelligence, and strength of humans developed in Greece. Greek art depicted the beauty of human beings as never before.

THE GREEKS INVENT THE CITY-STATE

After 800 B.C., a period lasting three hundred years known as the Archaic Age started in Greece. This period was followed by the Classical Age. At the beginning of the Archaic Age, numerous villages were scattered throughout the Greek territory. Some were of ancient origin; others had been created by newly settled populations. The head of each village was no more than a tribal leader, the head of the most important family in the village. Such a village king was not an absolute sovereign and did not hold all power in his hands. The principal members of other powerful families, the nobles, also shared in the power. Gradually, the importance of the kings decreased, and the nobles became the rulers of the growing villages. This form of power was called oligarchy. As they grew in size and population, many villages began to establish links with one another. Thus, new units of territory were formed, based on several villages and the surrounding countryside. These groups of villages, whose land was often extensively farmed, were the first step toward the creation of the polis or city-state. The polis was not a single town; several villages could be included within its domain, and one of them would become the dominant village. The main feature of the polis was that all the people living within its territory felt that they belonged to the same unit, not only a territorial unit, but also a political unit. Our word *politics* is derived from the *polis*.

An acropolis was built as a symbol of the new city-state, usually on a hill. On the acropolis, temples were erected, creating an important ceremonial place for all citizens.

Not far from the acropolis was a meeting area called the agora. It consisted of a square with houses around it. The agora formed the heart of the polis, becoming the centre for economic exchange. What makes it important in history is the fact that it was the hub of political life.

In the beginning, the agora was the meeting point for the heads of families. The members of the oligarchy would gather there to make decisions concerning the government of the city-state. They were landowners, very wealthy farmers who had servants. Peasants and traders who eventually acquired some wealth were also allowed to participate in political life.

In order to take part in political decisions, it was necessary to be a citizen. This privilege was extended to all the people who were born within the territory of the polis. Foreigners who settled in a Greek city-state could never become citizens. Women were citizens but did not have the freedom to take part fully in political life.

The Greeks invented a new form of political and social structure, the polis, or city-state. Town and country were combined in the new organization, at the heart of which was the acropolis, shown below.

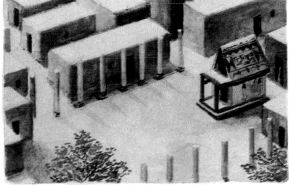

The agora was the meeting point for the people of the polis and was used as a market and assembly area. It was also a religious area, with temples and altars.

Below: a plan of the ancient agora of Calauria.

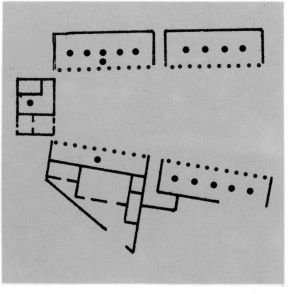

Nation and Homeland

In order to understand what a Greek state was, imagine a stretch of territory with a large valley, forested slopes, bottom pastures, fields, vineyards, and olive groves big enough to sustain ten thousand people. The territory also included a mountain or hill, which could be used as a shelter in case of attack, and a harbour for trade with neighbouring states. At times, the town was surrounded by defensive walls.

The city-state was born out of the passion its citizens felt for their independence. The city-states were independent entities with their own laws, currency, systems of weights and measures, and sacred territorial marker stones.

Most important of all, the citizens of these city-states had faith in their protector gods and goddesses, in their ancestors, and in a primal father. These beliefs, in the supernatural and traditional roots of their city, created an identity for the state and its people.

1. Eretria
2. Ephesus
3. Rhodes
4. Corinth
5. Chalcis

MOTHER CITY

COLONY

25
33
37
26
38
35
31
18
32
11 12
20
15
13
19
30
14 17
39
16 24

The founding of a colony was always associated with religious rituals. One of the most important procedures was the construction of the Prytaneum, the sacred building inside which sacred fire constantly burned.

11. Metapontum
12. Tarentum
13. Croton
14. Agrigentum
15. Sybaris

THE EXPANSION OF GREECE: HELLAS

In the early 700s B.C., Greece began to expand and establish settlements along the coasts of the Aegean Sea, the Black Sea, and the central and western Mediterranean Sea.

For two hundred years, the Greek world grew constantly larger. It eventually clashed with Phoenicians and later with Carthaginians, who gained dominion over sea trade.

Why Colonize?

Various reasons prompted the beginning of

Greek colonization: they included population growth, political oppression, social unrest, the need to conquer new markets and new territories, and the drive for heroic adventure. In the beginning, colonization was carried on by groups of farmers. Later, it became controlled by the city-states. Each Greek colony was

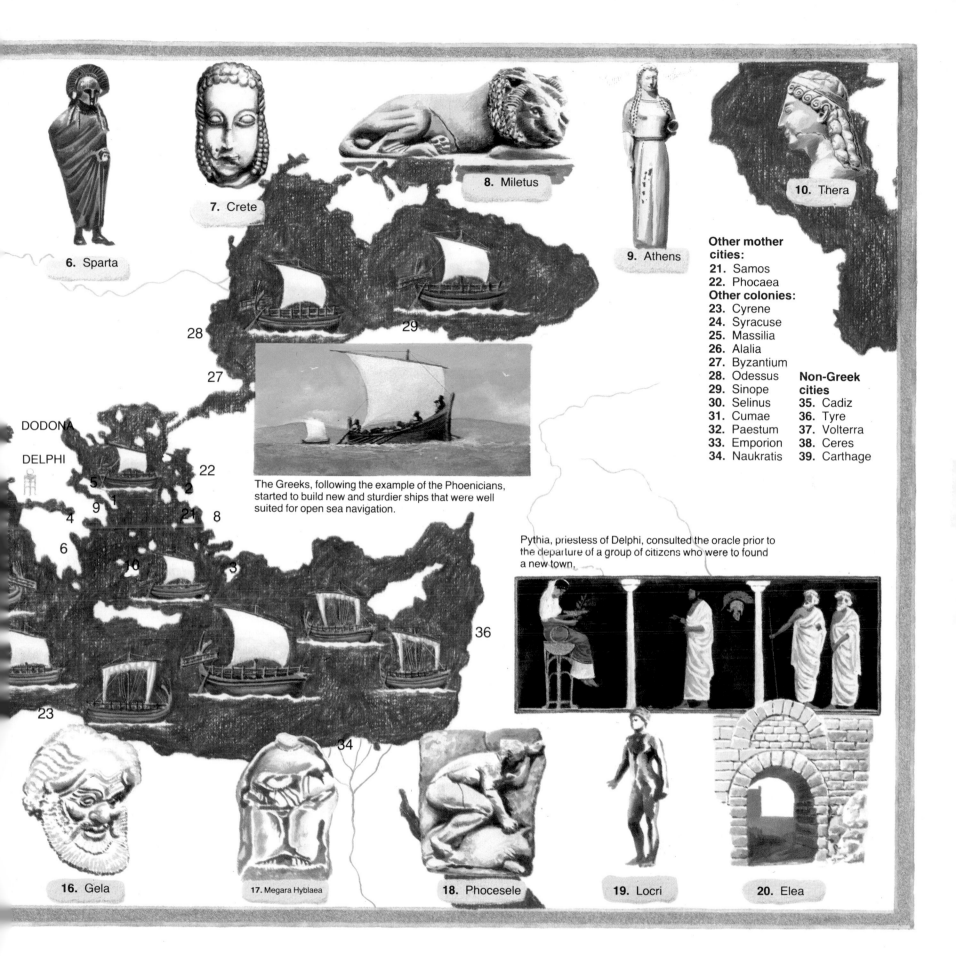

6. Sparta
7. Crete
8. Miletus
9. Athens
10. Thera

Other mother cities:
21. Samos
22. Phocaea
Other colonies:
23. Cyrene
24. Syracuse
25. Massilia
26. Alalia
27. Byzantium
28. Odessus
29. Sinope
30. Selinus
31. Cumae
32. Paestum
33. Emporion
34. Naukratis

Non-Greek cities:
35. Cadiz
36. Tyre
37. Volterra
38. Ceres
39. Carthage

DODONA

DELPHI

The Greeks, following the example of the Phoenicians, started to build new and sturdier ships that were well suited for open sea navigation.

Pythia, priestess of Delphi, consulted the oracle prior to the departure of a group of citizens who were to found a new town.

16. Gela
17. Megara Hyblaea
18. Phocesele
19. Locri
20. Elea

politically independent and had its own laws.

Hellas

Mother cities and their colonies together did not form an empire, for they did not have a common government. Yet the colonization process made the city-states even stronger. The group of city-states which gradually developed in Greece, together with the colonies in other territories, is called Hellas. The Greek people in the colonies maintained their language and religion, and retained strong commercial and cultural relationships with Greece. The Greek language had developed in ancient times. Through colonization, the Greek language spread throughout the shores of the Mediterranean. Soon Greek became the prominent language in many trading cities. The religious bonds between the colonies and Greece were also strongly felt by the people living there.

METICS

Though they could not be citizens, foreigners, called metics, were indispensable to the life of the Greek city-state. They were prominent in commerce and technical work, and were sometimes involved in military duties. They

could draw up contracts and be judged by tribunals, so they had civil rights. However, since they could not take part in elections or be elected, they did not have the same political rights as Greek citizens.

OLIGARCHY

FARMERS MERCHANTS, ARTISANS

FOREIGNERS (metics)

FOREIGNERS (metics)

POOR FARMERS
People who did not always have enough land to sustain themselves and their families

THETES
People with no personal possessions who lived precariously or were in the service of wealthy families

SLAVES
The descendants of subjugated people, poor citizens enslaved because of debts, or foreign people who had been defeated and enslaved

This diagram illustrates the structure of Greek society

1. *Left:* An electrum, a gold and silver alloy coin with a lion head from Smyrna, 575 B.C.. *Right:* A silver coin dedicated to the river god Gela, from Greater Greece, approximately 480 B.C. **2.** A blacksmith and his tools are depicted on an amphora from Attica, end of the sixth century B.C. **3.** An example of the Archaic alphabet. **4.** This inscription on a stone forms a list of names. It is from Thera, and dates from the second half of the sixth century B.C.

The Birth of Currency

Starting in the seventh century B.C., currency began to be used for commercial trade in the Mediterranean region. Before the introduction of currency, barter was the means of trade. The kingdoms of Asia Minor were the first to use coins, soon followed by the Greek city-states. Coins were made of precious metals (gold, silver, or bronze), had a determined weight, and were marked with the symbol of the king or of the town where they were struck. The value of the coins was based upon the trust which the wealth and power of the issuing country inspired. In a very short time, currency gained enormous importance in the economy. It was accepted by all, both on the market and as payment for work. The use of coins spread rapidly and even reached lands where the issuing country had no real power. A strong currency attracted merchants and goods, improved the economic health of the issuing country, and extended the influence of that country.

Technology and the Alphabet

During the Archaic Age, a great deal of progress was made in technology. The working of iron, which had been developed some centuries earlier, was improved and became widespread. More and more farm and artisan tools as well as weaponry were produced. Heavier ploughs and better farming equipment made possible the cultivation of wet lands which could not be farmed before, resulting in an expansion of agriculture. This caused the population explosion which led to colonization. New iron tools and the imitation of Phoenician shipbuilding techniques contributed to the improvement in the art of shipbuilding. The new ships were strong enough to sail across open seas. In cultural life, a major innovation of the period was the introduction of the phonetic alphabet, derived from the Phoenician alphabet. The main feature of this alphabet was that each character corresponded to a particular sound. The Phoenicians wrote only the consonants; the Greeks added the vowels, creating the first complete alphabet.

SOCIAL LIFE IN GREECE

Monarchy to Oligarchy

In the city-state, the king remained as a figurehead, often considered as a superior among equals.

However, the essence of monarchy no longer existed. A new form of government called *oligarchy* replaced the monarchy. It was formed by the heads of the most important families – landowners, cattle owners, and copper mine owners. They were the representatives of the power-centres of the state economy. This class of aristocrats has been called by various names. The most highly regarded were the *knights*. These aristocratic warriors owned horses which enabled them to ride into battle wearing bronze armour. Each mounted warrior had a shield, a helmet, a cuirass, metal leg covers (greaves), a long lance, and a short sword. The poor farmers, on the other hand, had to fight on foot, and were armed only with a short javelin.

Changes in Society

Between 700 and 600 B.C., an economic revolution occurred in Greek society. It was caused by the discovery and colonization of new worlds in the Mediterranean region, the widespread use of currency, iron tools and weapons, and population growth. The owners of fields, pastures, vineyards, and mines, who before had gained new wealth by fighting, were now able to enrich themselves through new commercial activities.

In some towns the landowners remained the dominant class. Elsewhere, especially in the colonies and on the islands, trade created a new wealthy merchant class. Sometimes, the sons and daughters of declining aristocratic families would marry those of rich merchants, thereby narrowing the difference between the old and new aristocracy. The middle class was also gaining in economic power. It was composed of farmers, artisans, and merchants and these people began to play an increasingly significant role in the life of the city-state.

Political Institutions

Government had a different structure in each individual city. However, there were some common political features.

Assembly. The assembly, which had various names (ecclesia, alia, apella), was composed of a varying number of individuals forming the so-called group of "active citizens". Decisions were hardly ever made within the assembly. Most often the assembly would merely approve decisions made by the council or simply give advice on various issues.

Council. The council had greater powers than the assembly. It was a smaller group of people, usually formed by the most wealthy citizens. These were either the most powerful citizens, who had recently acquired wealth, or members of the major families.

Magistrature. Ruling the city involved various tasks. At the time of the monarchy, the king was advised by a council. Members of the council with special duties were called magistrates, and made up a magistrature. Some magistrates were the heads of the council, such as the *ephors* in Sparta or the *demiurges* in various other cities. Others attended to special functions, such as the supervision of public works, and the performance of religious ceremonies.

The Tyrants

The creation of a new middle class made possible the introduction of the hoplites into the army. It also caused increasing criticism of the role of the aristocracy.

Greek society was structured into various social classes. The servant-class were slaves. The thetes were poor peasants. Above them were the foreigners or metics, both poor and rich, who were constantly trying to gain further rights. Even though foreigners were never allowed to acquire Greek citizenship, they gradually gained more and more power. Faced with such an unstable social situation, the ruling oligarchy had a very hard time trying to govern, due both to internal struggle and to pressure from the middle class. Sometimes, this situation was resolved by the appointment of a new supreme leader, the tyrant. The tyrant was a nobleman who took the government of the city-state into his hands during particularly difficult times. He did not have to obey the laws that applied to all the other citizens. Today, the word *tyrant* has a negative connotation, but this was not usually the case with the city-state tyrants, some of whom were very wise rulers. The tyrant, who had power over both the assembly and the council, had the power to alter the law. Some tyrants issued new, just laws and assisted the development of a democratic state. But others had no time for law-making and ruled in an arbitrary and violent way.

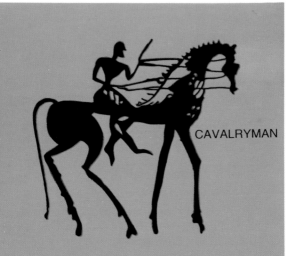

CAVALRYMAN

Changes in the Army: The Hoplites

As military techniques were modernized, new types of warriors called hoplites appeared. Each warrior wore a helmet and a cuirass and carried a round shield, a long spear, and a short sword. Most of the infantry was composed of merchants, artisans, and small landowners who could afford to buy the equipment. They formed the army of the city. Aristocratic chivalry lost much of its importance. Battles pivoted around the clashes of close ranks of foot-soldiers who fought in an orderly and unified manner, shoulder to shoulder, protecting each other with their shields. This sense of cohesion and order, of equal rights and shared responsibilities, was a basic expression of the guiding principle of life in the Greek city-state.

HOPLITES IN BATTLE

Athens, the largest city-state in Attica, was founded on democracy. Every adult male citizen had the right to participate in political life. *Inset:* The structure of Athenian government.

ATHENS AND SPARTA

Athens Dominates Attica

Attica was a region of Greece that had always been ruled by people of Ionian descent. It was unified under the hegemony of Athens and became a city-state. Attica was a large, principally agricultural region, ruled by a powerful group of aristocratic landowners. When the power of the kings declined, Athens was ruled by the aristocracy. In its social structure, the difference between nobles and the lower class was clearly marked.

Economic Problems

The economic situation in Athens was becoming increasingly difficult, and around the end of the seventh century B.C., dissatisfaction was common among the people of Attica. Changing ways of life meant that the nobles who owned most of the land (grain farms) faced new economic competition. Some of the wealthier farmers had begun to cultivate

vineyards, fruit trees, olive trees, and grow trees for timber. In addition, they successfully traded their produce. The poor farmers, on the other hand, were continually forced to borrow money in order to survive. A long chain of debt accumulated through the course of the years, forcing many farmers to lose their land to rich creditors.

The Tyrant of Athens

The social disorders caused by these problems were solved by the noble Peisistratus, who ruled as a tyrant without resorting to violence. He established the basis for further reforms which proved satisfactory to the majority of people in Athens. During his government, Peisistratus also succeeded in extending the hegemony of Athens over the island of Salamis, over some islands of the Aegean Sea, and along the shores of the Hellespont. After his death in 527, his sons Hippias and Hipparchus tried to hold on to

THE POLITICAL CONSTITUTION OF ATHENS

The Reforms of Solon

The Athenian statesman Solon (about 630 B.C.-560 B.C.) issued a decree prohibiting loans based on the financial security of people or their land holdings. He did not redistribute the land equally but divided Athenian society into four classes, defined according to the amount of revenue from the land they owned. The people belonging to the first two classes were the aristocrats, and had access to the main political positions. The magistrates, treasurers and archons were chosen from this group. Citizens belonging to the third (middle) class served in the army as hoplites. There were two systems of democratic control. All male citizens took part in the assembly, and each had the right to vote. In

CLASSES BY REVENUE

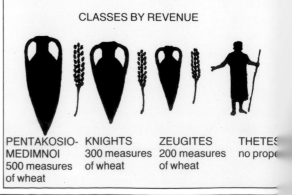

PENTAKOSIO-MEDIMNOI
500 measures of wheat

KNIGHTS
300 measures of wheat

ZEUGITES
200 measures of wheat

THETES
no prope

ΣΓΑΡΤΑ

The male citizens of Sparta trained constantly for war. All adult males underwent military training, which imposed strict discipline. The men drilled and ate together.

Inset: The structure of Spartan government

addition, each male citizen could be part of the *heliaea*, the tribunal of the people, which judged crimes against the community, even if the accused were members of the noble class.

The Reform of Cleisthenes

The two fundamental objectives of the reform of Cleisthenes (about 570 B.C. – after 510 B.C.) were to decrease the powers of the great noble families and to ease the divisions between the various classes of citizens. He divided Attica into three geographical and economic regions – the mountainous poor area to the north (Diacria), the rich central plain (Pedia), and the coastal area (Paralia), where commercial, artisan, and maritime activities flourished. Each region was divided into districts, which were grouped into threes to form a tribe. There was a total of ten tribes. Being the result of a territorial division, the tribe was less tightly connected to the family group than ever before. Each tribe had to provide an army of hoplites and elected a *strategos* as its leader. Each tribe sent fifty representatives to Athens, to take part in the council of the five hundred (*boule*). The *ecclesia* was regularly summoned to check on the work of the council of the five hundred.

To protect the state against attempts of tyrants to seize power, a new sanction was introduced – ostracism. Citizens had the power to ban from Athens any individual suspected of plotting against the state.

power, but Hipparchus was murdered, and Hippias was eventually overthrown with the help of the Spartans. Athens then developed a democratic government under Cleisthenes. Democracy was to continue in Athens under the leadership of Pericles.

The Dorians

When the migrating Dorians reached the Peloponnesus, they conquered the eastern region called Laconia and the Achaeans who lived there. The Dorians never integrated with the local population. They remained an armed, separate minority.

The Military Democracy of Sparta

The Dorians never ceased to consider themselves an occupation army in Laconia, and this greatly affected their way of life. Freed from the burden of cultivating the land, which was done for them by the subdued local people,

they were constantly armed and on the defensive. Sparta, the only city-state in Laconia, had a militarist organization. Its inhabitants were always ready to defend themselves against an enemy, both from outside and within their borders.

Political Life in Sparta

The political structure in Sparta was designed to avoid the possibility of predominance of one individual over all the others. Tyranny was strongly rejected. According to tradition, around 700 B.C., Lycurgus gave Sparta a body of laws to regulate its society. The people of Sparta were supposedly the first among the Greeks to have a complete body of written laws.

Political life was based on the *apella*, the assembly of armed men. Most of the power, however, was in the hands of the *gerousia*, a council formed of twenty-eight *gerontes*, or elders.

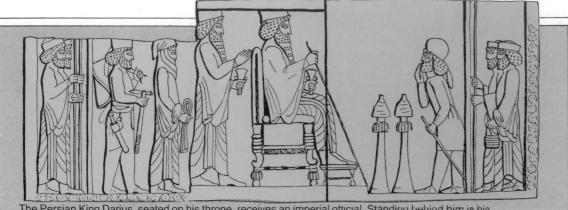

The Persian King Darius, seated on his throne, receives an imperial official. Standing behind him is his son, Xerxes, a civil servant, and a bodyguard. This illustration was taken from a bas-relief at Persepolis.

THE PERSIAN WARS

The Persian Empire in Asia Minor

In the mid-sixth century B.C., the king of Persia made his state into a great power. Persian influence swallowed the Greek colonies of Asia Minor. The Persian political system was different from that of the city-states of Greece. The eastern empire was a vast territory inhabited by various peoples, all under the sovereignty of the emperor. The Persian presence in the Aegean Sea facilitated trade with the East and represented a 'superpower' presence from which military and political help could be obtained. The Ionia region, inhabited by Greeks, had become a province of the Persian empire. Its rulers were tyrants who were faithful to the emperor. In Greece, the outer territories sided with the Persians, while the city-states remained divided on whether to oppose or accept Persian dominance.

The Ionic Rebellion

In 500 B.C., the tyrant of Miletus rebelled against Persia and installed a democratic government. The rebellion spread to many other Ionic towns, whose inhabitants were also under the economic and political control of the Persians. The Ionians received some help from Athens but were defeated.

At this point, the Persians were interested in Greek territory not only for the wealth it contained, but also because of the political and military threat posed by the Greek towns, first and foremost Athens. In 490, the Persians destroyed Eretria from the sea and swarmed into the plain of Marathon, about 40 kilometres from Athens. There the hoplites of Athens, lead by Miltiades, though greatly outnumbered, defeated the Persians and forced them to retreat.

Xerxes and the End of the Persian Wars

King Darius's son, Xerxes, succeeded his father in 486 and led expeditions against Greece, both by sea and by land. The Greeks were defeated in the battle of Thermopylae in 480. But the Athenian fleet lead by Themistocles met the Persian ships in a great naval battle off Salamis, near Athens, and defeated them. The following year, at Plataea, the Greek army defeated the Persian army once and for all.

This map shows the routes of the Persian wars. The red broken line indicates the sea route of the first Persian war. The war against Athens was started by Darius in 490 B.C. The Athenians defeated his army at the Battle of Marathon. In 480, an expedition led by Xerxes attacked the Greek towns, both by land and by sea (solid red line and dotted red line respectively). The expedition of 480 was driven back by the Greeks as a result of their victories at Salamis and Plataea.

Persian expedition of 490 B.C.
Persian expedition of 480 B.C.
Route followed by the fleet of Xerxes

Aegean Sea
Thessaly
Thebes
Plataea
Athens
Marathon
Eretria
Celaenae
Miletus
Salamis
Sparta
Mediterranean Sea

The great ruler Pericles, who led Athens during the period of its greatest splendour.

This picture shows Pericles about to enter the Assembly held in the Pnyx, a special amphitheatre on a hill facing the Acropolis in Athens.

THE AGE OF PERICLES

Pericles and Athens

Pericles was born into a wealthy aristocratic Athenian family. Yet he supported the democratic party. Under his rule, Athens flourished and became an artistic, cultural, and political centre admired by all the Greek world.

Foreign Policy

Pericles led his army to victory in numerous wars. As a result, Athens became a true empire. The Athenians imposed general regulations concerning the government of towns under their control and the currency. At times they sent out law-enforcers to exert their power over the most rebellious cities. The economic control of Athens is evident in the use of currency. Athenian coins, the famous "owls of Athens" (tetradrachms), were the only currency used in trade between the cities. The Mediterranean became a vast market for the benefit of the Greeks. However, trading partners could still not obtain political influence, for Athens was still ruled like a city-state. Only the children of Athenian parents could be citizens of Athens.

The Splendour of Athens

Athens had an aggressive foreign policy, but its internal policy was highly democratic. Everything was arranged so that the highest possible number of citizens could take part in political life. A lottery method was applied for choosing most of the men who served as magistrates. All those who held public positions were paid for their duties.

Great commercial wealth accumulated from the revenues Athens collected from its empire. Pericles decided that such abundance should be used to remedy the damage caused by the Persians. He started major public works projects. The Acropolis, the agora, and the road leading to the harbour were rebuilt. Athens became the main cultural centre of Greece. It was a meeting point for famous artists, writers and philosophers.

The Peloponnesian War

After the death of Pericles, Athens continued its expansionary policy. In 415, B.C., the Athenians organized an expedition to Sicily, which was to end in defeat. The Peloponnesian War, between the Athenian empire and the Peloponnesian League under Spartan leadership, began in 431 B.C. and ended in 404 B.C. with a victory by the Spartans. They forced Athens to reduce drastically the size of its fleet, to give up all of its territories except for Attica and Salamis, and to destroy the fortifications of the harbour at Piracus. The Spartan army occupied Athens and supported the violent rule of the so-called Thirty Tyrants. These tyrants harshly persecuted the proponents of democracy. The end of democracy in Athens was a sign of a widespread crisis throughout Greece. The city-states were no longer able to coexist peacefully, and disagreements between them made all the states weak and unstable.

A silver coin, known as the "owl of Athens". The owl was the symbol of commerce. The olive leaves indicated the main agricultural product of the city-state.

A Greek coin from Sicily, showing the prow of a warship.

Part of the western frieze of the Parthenon. It depicts a procession of knights.

The Greeks painted their statues and reliefs (right) but, with time, the colour has worn away (left).

Athens and the harbour at Piraeus.

THE ACROPOLIS OF ATHENS

Under Pericles, Athens became a treasury of architecture and art. Phidias, the most famous sculptor of the time, was given the task of restoring the Acropolis and of decorating the temple of Athena, which is called the Parthenon, with friezes (ornate bands) and sculptures. Phidias also sculpted the statue of Athena, which was cast in bronze and placed on the Acropolis. A monumental entrance with a double colonnade, called the Propylaea, was erected. The Erechtheum, a temple dedicated to Athena and Poseidon, was also restored.

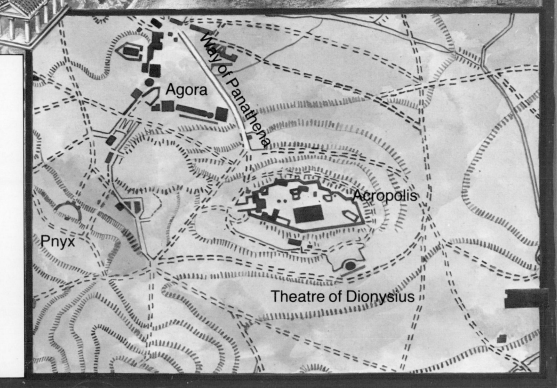

The Monuments of the Acropolis

1. The temple of Athena Nike
2. The gallery of paintings
3. The Propylaea, the monumental entrance to the Acropolis
4. The bronze statue of Athena Promachos by Phidias
5. The sanctuary of Artemis Brauronia
6. The Chalkoteki
7. The Parthenon, a vast temple which housed the statue of Athena
8. The temple of Pandrosos with the sacred olive tree
9. The Erechtheum built on the site of more ancient temples
10. The great altar of Athena
11. The enclosure of Zeus Polieus and Bukoleion, where barley, wheat, and a sacred ox were offered to the gods according to an ancient ritual
12. The temple of Pandion
13. The theatre of Dionysius

Right: Sites of important monuments and public buildings in the centre of Athens at the time of Pericles.

Way of Panathena

Agora

Pnyx

Acropolis

Theatre of Dionysius

THE GREEKS IN THE MEDITERRANEAN

Greater Greece and Sicily

The Greek colonies became more splendid and richer in art and culture than Greece itself. The first colonies established by the Greeks were Pithecusae (on the island of Ischia) and Cyme in the Campania region. The towns of Messina, Rhegion, Leontini, Catania and Himera were founded shortly afterwards. The settlers made wise use of the resources of the territory (tin, copper, and bronze). In a short time, they gained control over much of the sea trade going west through the Straits of Messina. Other Greek settlers carried on the colonization process. They were Megarians,

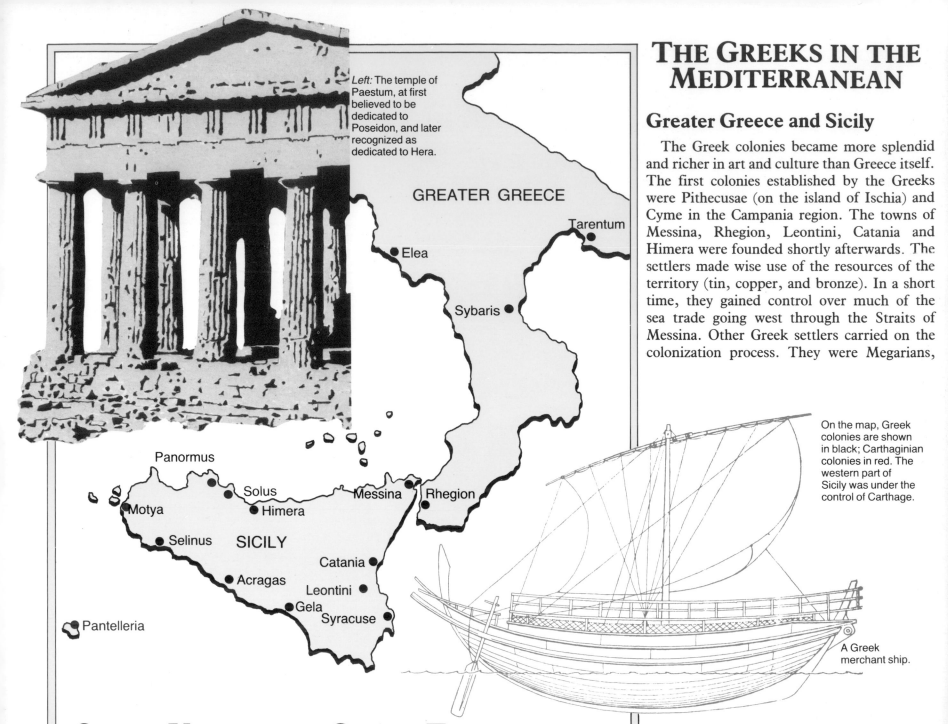

Left: The temple of Paestum, at first believed to be dedicated to Poseidon, and later recognized as dedicated to Hera.

GREATER GREECE

Tarentum

Elea

Sybaris

Panormus

Solus

Motya

Himera

Messina

Rhegion

Selinus

SICILY

Catania

Acragas

Leontini

Gela

Syracuse

Pantelleria

On the map, Greek colonies are shown in black; Carthaginian colonies in red. The western part of Sicily was under the control of Carthage.

A Greek merchant ship.

SICILY UNDER THE GREAT TYRANTS

A new form of government originated in Sicily. It was less democratic than the government of the Greek city-state, less despotic than the governments of the eastern states. Its head was a lord who ruled over the court and the army. This form of government was called tyranny. The tyrant Dionysius ruled over a large stronghold close to present-day Syracuse. Immigrants and mercenary soldiers found work in Syracuse and were granted the same political rights as the citizens of the town. All citizens were subject to the tyrants. Often the tyrants had the approval of the majority because they opposed the aristocratic class. The nobles wanted to revive oligarchic power, but were disunited since their various factions were in constant disagreement.

Syracuse became the largest city in the Greek world, and the capital of a vast territory. This territory came to include most of Sicily and numerous towns of southern Italy. Its influence was felt throughout the Mediterranean, and as far as northern Italy.

Syracuse was always at war with Carthage, the North African state which was to become the most important naval power in the Mediterranean before the rise of Rome. This constant state of war, both against Carthage and against the Etruscans in Italy, together with the desire of Syracuse to impose its power over various Greek towns, were practical reasons which justified the need for an efficient, if tyrannical, government.

Corinthians, Achaeans, Spartans and Cretans. In Sicily, they founded important towns such as Syracuse, Gela, Acragas and Selinus; in Greater Greece they founded Tarentum, Elea and Sybaris.

Contacts with Gaul

The Phocaeans, Greek traders renowned for their swift ships propelled by fifty rowers, reached the coast of Gaul (modern France). There, around 600 B.C., they founded the town of Massilia (Marseilles). The area was rich in tin, coral and salt, and was also in a favourable location for trade. The Phocaeans sought out trading bases where they could sell goods. In Marseilles, they entered into direct commercial competition with the Etruscans. The Etruscans had already established a growing exchange of metals and ceramics with the peoples living in southern France.

Even Carthage, which controlled the sea

The Greeks had fruitful contacts with other peoples throughout the Mediterranean. As well as trading goods, they dealt in art and other products of their culture. 1) Grain traders in the port of Marseilles; 2) Greek merchants offer a vase made in Greece to a Celtic aristocrat; 3) Greek ships; 4) Greek chariots; 5) a sea battle between Greeks and Carthaginians; 6) exchange of handicrafts between Greeks and Etruscans.

trade in the western Mediterranean, was affected by the presence of the Greeks. An important military event was the battle of Alalia (around 540 B.C.). Here the Etruscans and Carthaginians fought successfully together against the Greeks in order to defend their commercial dominion from the influence of the Phocaeans who had settled in Corsica.

Marseilles gradually obtained a vast maritime empire. Among its numerous colonies were Olbia, Antibes, Nice and other southern coastal towns. In this way, in spite of its limited size, it was able to spread its culture and commercial products along the valley of the River Rhône, into the heart of Celtic territory.

Greeks and Carthaginians in Iberia

Both Greeks and Carthaginians had had commercial bases in Iberia (Spain and Portugal) for a long time. In some cases, settlers came from their mother countries to create colonies. The Greeks were essentially merchants and established more or less permanent stopovers (*emporia*) or used existing bases. They would exchange their merchandise and leave again with a load of silver and other precious metals. A permanent colony was founded, with the help of the people of Marseilles, on the Spanish coast north of the

Ebro River. It was called Emporion (modern Ampurias).

The Mediterranean and Europe

From 800 B.C. to 300 B.C., trade activities and the settlement of colonies brought about minglings of peoples and cultures which had a far-reaching influence on the Mediterranean and on the whole of European civilization. The expansion of Greece and Carthage triggered extremely fast historical development. A common heritage developed. This gave great stimulus to the growth of local cultures, such as those of Italy and the Iberian peninsula. The growth of this unified Greek-influenced culture influenced the more distant regions of Europe, in particular bringing about great change in the Celtic world.

Left: An archaic sculpture placed within the Acropolis of Athens around 530 B.C.

A vase from Corinth (seventh-sixth century B.C.). Due to Eastern influence, the Greek vase painters began to use new decorative elements, such as this winged beast.

A temple is shown under construction. The heavy blocks of stone were transported with the help of special machinery. A winch was used to lift the sections of columns, and scaffolding allowed work on upper levels. *Top insert:* The technique employed in lifting heavy stone blocks in order to position them securely, one beside the other, made use of vertical and horizontal wedges. The tools used in sculpting stone were, as they are today, hammers and chisels, used first in rough shaping and then in fine finishing work.

THE ART OF GREECE

Greek art is divided into three periods—Archaic, Classical and Hellenistic. The most famous is the Classical period, which dates from the end of the Persian wars (480 B.C.) to the invasion of the Persian Empire by Alexander the Great (333-323 B.C.). Victory over the Persians played a major part in forming the new Greek mentality that created the art of the early and mature Classical periods. The conquests of Alexander and the spread of Greek culture in Asia marked the final steps in the process of this social and emotional transformation.

Archaic Period to Early Classical Period

The Classical period in Greek art was preceded by the Archaic period, which dated from the seventh century B.C. to shortly before the Persian wars. This first period is characterized by an artistic search for universal order. Statues of the period seem to be untouched by mere human events. On the other hand, the statues of the early Classical period (480-450 B.C.) tend to be more dramatic and associated with contemporary life.

Greek artists believed that the basis of human expression was *ethos* (the nature of people and their traditions, habits and morals) and *pathos* (people's spontaneous reaction to experience). One of the best examples of the expression of ethos is in the bronze figure known as the Charioteer of Delphi. The serious, aristocratic self-control of this figure is an ideal representation of victory after a chariot race. During the early Classical period artists believed that harmony and order could be found in movement. Thus, sculpted or painted figures were depicted as reacting, moving or thinking.

In sculpture, an aspect of composition called *rythmos* became predominant. It froze movement, capturing an entire action within an instant. A typical example is the Discobolus, by the sculptor Myron, in which a discus thrower is represented split seconds before the discus leaves his hand.

Classical Period to Hellenistic Period

The value of symmetry was always appreciated in Greek art, and the classical period was the time of its highest expression. A work had to be composed of clearly definable parts, capable of bringing opposite forces into harmony. Symmetry is very finely expressed in the Parthenon. The building embodies the Greek humanist ideal, with its conviction that human reason will prevail and perfect the world. Its architecture and its sculptures, the work of the artist Phidias and his students, celebrate the values of the city and community.

The combination in architecture of the Doric and Ionic orders was one of the elements symbolizing Athenian ideals in the time of Pericles. The Doric order was associated with the solid simplicity of the descendants of Hercules in the Peloponnese, while the Ionic order expressed luxury and refinement. Naturally, Pericles wanted both orders to be present and brought into harmony in the art of Athens. The art of the period which followed the Peloponnesian War (from 431 to 404 B.C.) reflected the disintegration of this artistic and philosophical ideal, and the disillusionment with the values of the city-state. The leading

The *Discobolus* by the sculptor Myron. This figure illustrates the sense of movement expressed by artists of the early classical period.

The bronze *Charioteer of Delphi* (478-474 B.C.) wears the typical charioteer's tunic, belted in a distinctive way. The statue is a superb example of the nobility of the human figure, as expressed in classical Greek art.

A vase decorated with red figures on a black background (Eretria, approximately 430 B.C.). The work of a skilled painter, it depicts a woman holding a ribbon in one hand and a box in the other.

At Olympia, in the workshop of Phidias, craftsmen apply the last gold plate to the statue of Zeus soon to be installed in the Temple of Zeus. This huge statue, one of the Wonders of the Ancient World, is now lost. Its appearance can be imagined, thanks to written descriptions and some archaeological finds. It was built of ivory and gold plates applied to a wooden internal frame. *Top insert:* The workshop which Pheidias constructed to build the statue was carefully sited so that the light entered its windows illuminating the god.

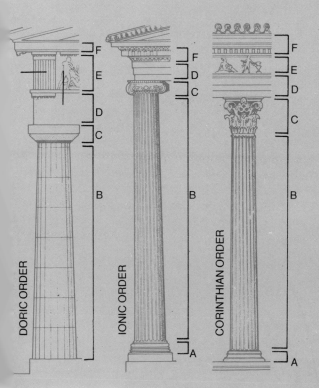

The Architectural Orders

Greek architecture was composed of vertical elements, columns, which supported horizontal elements, trabeations. Trabeations included lintels (**D**), friezes (**E**), and cornices (**F**). Buildings are placed in one of three classical orders.

THE DORIC ORDER is the most ancient. Its columns have no pedestals and have twenty grooves; the length of the shaft (**B**) is four to six times the diameter of the base. The frieze has vertical grooves, or triglyphs (**G**) alternating with ornamental bas-reliefs called metope (**H**).

THE IONIC ORDER with its typical voluted capitals originated in Asia Minor in the sixth century B.C. Its columns have twenty-four grooves, divided by cinctures; the total length of the shaft is generally nine times the diameter of the base of the column.

THE CORINTHIAN ORDER has a capital decorated with acanthus leaves. The lintel is almost always surmounted by friezes. Usually the height of the column is ten times the diameter of the base of the shaft.

sculptors of this time were Praxiteles, Scopa, and Lysippus.

In the following centuries, art increasingly reflected the experience of each person as an individual. The new style was called Hellenistic. Pathos received more attention than ethos, which no longer expressed the ideals of the community. Artists now explored personal emotions such as pain, tenderness, and humour, concentrating gesture and elegance of shape.

Building Techniques

The Greeks had acquired great skill in building. This is evident in temples, which are the principal achievements of Greek architecture, in city planning, and in public buildings such as theatres, stadiums and gymnasiums. The techniques and methods of construction were highly developed. Plans were drawn up by workers, each with a specialized responsibility. Machines for building included wheels, rollers, levers, winches and pulleys.

21

THE HEROES

1 2 3 4

THE GAMES

5 6 7 8

THE MYSTERY CULTS

9 10 11

THE CULT OF THE DEAD

12

THE HEROES: **1)** Ajax carries the slain Achilles. These two heroes of the epic poem, the *Iliad*, were famous for their courage in battle. **2)** From the *Odyssey*, Ulysses, epitome of human ingenuity and endurance, escapes from the giant Polyphemus. **3)** Theseus, the mythical king of Athens, established order and unity on his return to his homeland. **4)** A typical representation of Hercules, the invincible hero who was made a god after his death. He is shown wearing a lion skin.

THE GAMES: **5)** An ox is brought to be sacrificed prior to the opening of the games. **6)** An athlete long jumping. **7)** A footrace between runners naked save for helmets and shields. **8)** Throwing the javelin.

THE MYSTERY CULTS: **9)** The cult of Dionysus inspired the figures on ancient vases. A priestess distributes wine. **10)** Two young men carry a special vessel for the new wine. **11)** Dionysus holds a cup in his hand.

THE CULT OF THE DEAD: **12)** At a funeral feast, the family of the deceased offers milk, bread, and other food, while a lamb is prepared for sacrifice.

Opposite page: Mount Olympus, home of the gods. There were twelve principal deities – Zeus, the strongest of all the Gods; Hera, his wife; Poseidon, the god of the sea; Athena, the protector of fortresses and towns as well as the goddess of wisdom; Apollo, the god of youth and the healing song; Artemis, the goddess of animals and the wilderness as well as of the hunt; Aphrodite, the goddess of love; Hermes, the god of cleverness and the gods' winged messenger; Demeter, the goddess of crops; Dionysus, the god of wine and intoxication; Hephaestus, god of artisans and of fire; and Ares, the god of war.

THE RELIGION OF THE GREEKS

We think of Greek religion as wholly identified with the gods of Mount Olympus. But other deities were also respected. Each family, for example, could have its own god. Each town had its own god, as did each occupation or art. Failure to honour the gods could result in the grave accusation of impiety. The Greeks also held many sites, animals and plants as sacred.

The Oracles

The Greeks were anxious to know about the future. They particularly looked for signs of divine fury, which they tended to see in unusual or exceptional events or in natural phenomena such as eclipses of the sun, thunder or lightning. The gift of prophecy had been respected since ancient times. It was seen as the skill of communicating the will of the gods to people. The most famous oracle or mouthpiece of the divine will was the prophetess of Delphi in the temple of Apollo. Such attempts to see into the future and to understand the will of the gods showed how much the Greeks sought to establish communication with the gods.

The Cult of the Dead

Some deities inhabited Hades, the shadowy underworld. The cult associated with this universe of darkness is redolent with the fears the Greeks felt about the horrors that awaited them in the afterlife. Many rituals were intended to avert the possible revenge of the dead.

Heroes and Games

Men who had done great deeds were highly respected as the 'sons of the gods'. Such people became heroes. The most famous hero was Hercules. Athletic competitions were often part of the cult of heroes, and were much more than merely sports events.

Greek Myths

The Greek word *mythos* means "word" and comes from the Indo-European *mudh*, which means "to reflect" or "to consider". The most ancient texts used the word *mythos* to indicate a story concerning the gods.

Homer, who (though nothing is known about him, or her) probably lived in the eighth century B.C. wrote two great poems – the *Iliad*, an epic about the Trojan War, and the *Odyssey*, which narrates the deeds of Telemachus and Ulysses. In these long story-poems, the gods are depicted as forces that intervene in the lives of people. Hesiod probably lived in the 700s B.C. He wrote *The Works and Days*, a poem dedicated to the earth, and *Theogony*, which tells of the origins of gods and earthly things. Homer and Hesiod collected stories no doubt retold for generations. Poets were to sing of these myths in later times, and they were to be the inspiration for the famous Greek tragedies.

In later centuries, religious thought, philosophical research and literary activities dealt with the myths, at times criticizing them. From the late 600s B.C., philosophy attempted to provide a rational explanation of the world. The word *mythos* was to be replaced by *logos*, also meaning "word" and "thought". Logos was considered the spiritual principle which permeates all things. Plato was to give a new interpretation of the myths in order to provide people with a religious, moral and political education.

Until the coming of Christianity, Homer was considered a poet who expressed, with his myths, a revelation taken from a divine source. Thus, the myths introduced people to religious mysteries. Later, myths were regarded in various ways, either as the poetic expressions of historical events or as a means of understanding natural phenomena.

Today, myths are regarded as sacred stories which express poetically beliefs concerning fundamental situations related to humans – their origin, death, hope and the relationship between humans and gods. Myths do not relate historical facts, though sometimes they originated from real events. Myths express a consciousness of the human condition, a reflection of a truth that goes beyond the simple facts of history.

The Mysteries

The mysteries were secret ceremonies of very ancient origin. In them the sacred truths of myth were revealed. The mysteries were hopeful, and told of the possibility of life after death, not in Hades, which was sad and dark, but instead a peaceful existence. The best-known mystery cult was the cult of Dionysus.

The Gods of Mount Olympus

On Mount Olympus, home of the gods, Zeus ruled. The gods were unpredictable, and their often erratic relations with the human world were a source of literary inspiration.

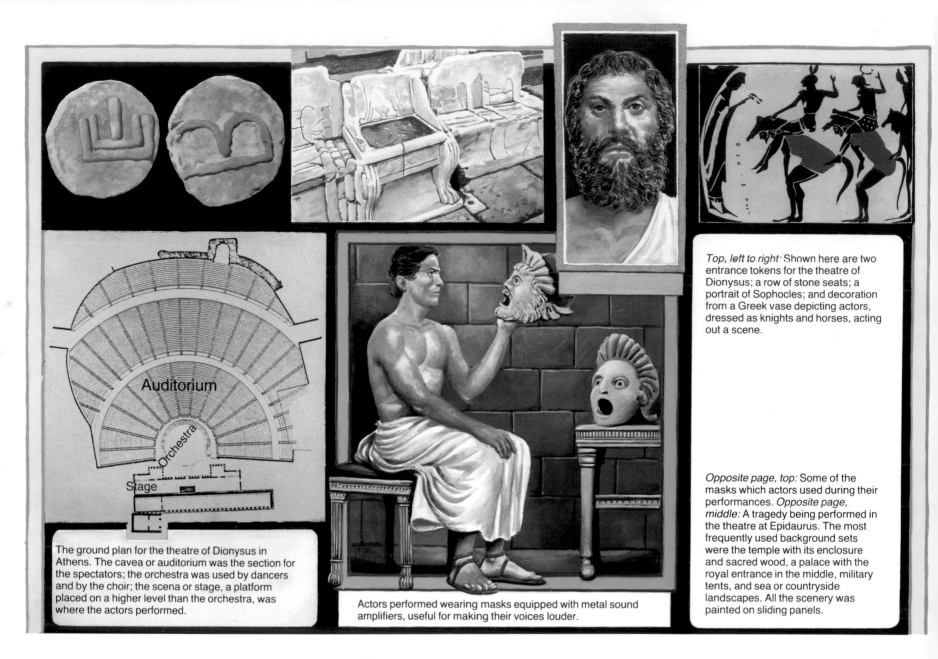

The ground plan for the theatre of Dionysus in Athens. The cavea or auditorium was the section for the spectators; the orchestra was used by dancers and by the choir; the scena or stage, a platform placed on a higher level than the orchestra, was where the actors performed.

Actors performed wearing masks equipped with metal sound amplifiers, useful for making their voices louder.

Top, left to right: Shown here are two entrance tokens for the theatre of Dionysus; a row of stone seats; a portrait of Sophocles; and decoration from a Greek vase depicting actors, dressed as knights and horses, acting out a scene.

Opposite page, top: Some of the masks which actors used during their performances. *Opposite page, middle:* A tragedy being performed in the theatre at Epidaurus. The most frequently used background sets were the temple with its enclosure and sacred wood, a palace with the royal entrance in the middle, military tents, and sea or countryside landscapes. All the scenery was painted on sliding panels.

GREEK THEATRE

Tragedies and Comedies

The Greek drama was one of the Greeks' greatest artistic legacies. It was a form of artistic expression capable of involving and deeply moving an audience. First came tragedy. Later, comedy was invented. These two forms of theatre greatly influenced the development of the drama in the West, up to the modern day.

The Origins of Tragedy: A Religious Ceremony

According to tradition, the first tragedy was played in Athens during the sixty-first Olympic Games (536-533 B.C.). In front of the audience gathered in the cavea, a sacrifice was offered to Dionysus, followed by dances. Lyrics sung by the choir alternated with mixed parts, where the actor could either alternate with the chorus or recite a monologue. These pieces were generally preceded by a prologue and by an entrance song performed by the choir. The event ended with a closing song. The choir played the most important role in the show. Later, the parts performed by the choir tended to become detached from the narration of the plot and were basically used as an expression of the feelings of the playwright.

Tragedy as a Public Ritual

Performances of tragedies were organized by the city government. Such dramas became public rituals celebrated during the festivals in honour of Dionysus. In the fifth century B.C. Athenian tragic drama reached new heights of public expression. The purpose of the drama was to present the citizens with a performance which would make them reflect upon their own experiences within the Athenian community.

ANTIGONE BY SOPHOCLES

Two brothers, Eteocles and Polynices, fought for the kingdom of Thebes to the point of killing each other. Creon, their uncle, ascended the throne and forbade the burial of the body of Polynices. Polynices's sister, Antigone, who believed in the religious tradition that the dead could not find peace until they were buried, disobeyed the order of the king and buried her brother. The king delivered a cruel sentence – Antigone was to be buried alive. Antigone's fiancé, Haemon, the son of

The Great Greek Dramatists

The tragedies of the three great Greek dramatists – Aeschylus, Sophocles, and Euripides – were not simply an expression of social life in the city-state. In their plays they examined the major themes at the heart of Greek civilization, such as the search for identity, and the passions and doubts of people.

The Comedy

The birth of comedy was also related to religious rituals, part of the cult of Dionysus.

In Athens, the performance of comedies always attracted large crowds. The audience, numbering up to fifteen thousand, took an active part, applauding and roaring. The most important writer of Greek comedy was Aristophanes (448-388 B.C.).

Menander (342-291 B.C.) created a sort of comedy which dealt with various stock characters – the miser, the complainer, the servant and others.

The Great Writers of Tragedy
AESCHYLUS (524-456 B.C.) wrote Prometheus Bound. Prometheus, a demi-god, was punished because he had stolen fire from the gods. SOPHOCLES (496-406 B.C.) did not have blind faith in the gods but defended them. Among his plays are *Oedipus Rex*, *Oedipus at Colonus*, and *Antigone*. EURIPIDES (480-406 B.C.) wrote *Hippolytus* in which Hippolytus dies while setting a trap for a goddess, and *Medea*, a tale of revenge. The Greeks believed the gods were capable of doing evil and that death put an end to everything.

DIONYSUS

Creon, followed Antigone into her tomb without his father's knowledge. Later, Creon, seized by doubt, ordered that the tomb be reopened. He found

Antigone, who had just committed suicide, and his son, who killed himself in front of Creon. Eurydice,

Haemon's mother, was overwhelmed by grief and also committed suicide.

Thales was the founder of the first Greek school of philosophy and was celebrated among his contemporaries because he predicted the eclipse of the sun during a battle on May 28, 585 B.C. He thought that the world was floating, suspended in water, which was the primeval life-substance.

PYTHAGORAS

The school of Pythagoras studied mathematics and intellectual training which developed clarity of thought. Mathematicians organized geometry into theorems and proofs. They studied arithmetic, the study of proportions, and music. The students of Pythagoras also studied astronomy, and concluded that the earth was a revolving sphere.

DEMOCRITUS

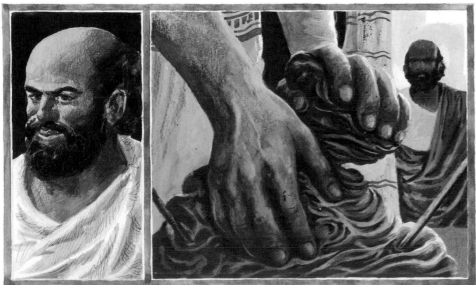

GREEK THOUGHT

The First School of Philosophy

In the sixth century, greater political stability in the Greek world was accompanied by economic prosperity. In Ionia in particular, peace generated great cultural energy. In Miletus, the southernmost of the Ionic towns, the first school of Greek philosophy flourished.

Thales of Miletus

Thales of Miletus, 640-548 B.C., founded the first Greek school of philosophy. He introduced mathematics and astronomy into Greece. He sought to identify the primeval substance from which everything derived, and thought he had found it in the element of water. His vision of the world was essentially practical, but did not completely exclude the presence of a creator or of an eternal life force.

Pythagoras and his followers

Pythagoras of Samos, an island near Miletus, lived a little later than Thales (from 580 to 500 B.C.) and taught in Croton in southern Italy. He created a community of followers, men and women, who made intellect their source of spiritual purification. Pythagoras was a student of mathematics and natural sciences. In his opinion, harmony was the ideal condition of the world and was attained by keeping just proportions of all things. The school of Pythagoras also strove to discover the primal element of reality. The later followers of Pythagoras stated that everything was composed of indivisible units or atoms. In this way, a new school of philosophy, called the atomistic school, was born.

Heraclitus of Ephesus

Heraclitus was an original thinker, whose teachings were most influential around 500 B.C. He lived on a mountain and looked for the one idea which would be capable of explaining everything. His philosophy was based on the idea that constant change ruled the world.

Parmenides of Elea

Parmenides lived in Elea in the Lucania region of Italy. Unlike Heraclitus, who insisted on the idea that everything was in motion, Parmenides was an advocate of the idea that things resisted change.

Democritus of Abdera

Abdera was an Ionic colony of Thrace. Here lived Democritus, an exponent of the atomistic school which developed from the school of Pythagoras. Democritus, however, never founded a school. He believed that all knowledge based on sensory perceptions is illusory, and that the only certainty comes from the intellect. According

Democritus formulated a theory that the world was composed only of atoms and empty space, and that the atoms united and separated according to an internal requirement as the clay is moulded in the sculptor's hands. The ideas of Democritus were among the most important in ancient science and remained a reference point for the scholars of later times.

to Democritus, the world (including people) was made of atoms which could be neither created nor destroyed but merely changed. This is a remarkably modern viewpoint.

The Sophists

By the second half of the fifth century B.C., Athens was the cultural capital of the Greek world. It was the centre of a vast intellectual movement, characterized by faith in the potential of human thought. The *Sophists*, a name which means "masters of wisdom", were an important element in this movement. Among their teachers was Protagoras, who lived a generation before Socrates. He declared that humans were the measure of all things. He denied the existence of any absolute truth, but stated that there were only specific truths which were valid for certain people in particular situations.

Socrates

Socrates investigated human nature, looking for true wisdom. But he soon arrived at the conclusion that he could only ask questions; that his wisdom was that he didn't know anything and his only teaching was about the art of examining ideas. The true virtue, for Socrates, was reached through the search for reason which opened the way to universal truth, the conceptual truth.

The personality of Socrates was described with admiration by his students, among them Plato and Xenophon. Part of Socrates's method was to invite anyone into discussion. In particular, he loved to teach young people. He used a method which was called Maieutic, which means the art of midwifery. Just as a midwife helps a child to come into the world, Socrates, with his continuous questions, helped students discover the truth inside their minds.

Plato

Plato (427-347 B.C.) founded an institution called the Academy in Athens. It was a kind of philosophical society to which both men and women were admitted. For Plato, philosophy was the science of ideas, which are the original and eternal models of all reality. He believed in the existence of a god who created all things and to whom people's souls are attracted through love. The supreme idea of Plato is the concept of good, the capacity for loving truth and acting in accordance with truth.

Plato founded the Academy, a meeting place for young scholars and philosophers. At the heart of his teachings, Plato placed the examination of the relationship between human experience and ideas.

Aristotle

Aristotle (384-322 B.C.) was an illustrious pupil of Plato. He also taught Alexander the Great, after which he returned to Athens to found a school dedicated to Apollo Lyceum, the god of shepherds. The school was called the Lyceum and was endowed by Alexander. According to Aristotle, humans have an active, rational capability. This allows them to understand the cause and effect that sets everything in motion. Art and thought must grasp the essential form of everything. This form is found in matter through sensory perception. Happiness comes through understanding of goodness, seen in the practice of virtue. For Plato, politics was the science of collective happiness. The main characteristic of Aristotle's work is the systematic ordering of all the knowledge of his time.

Aristotle's philosophy tried to explain the fundamentals of reality. He defined the way we think, and he introduced the concept of syllogism. Syllogism is a form of logical reasoning that allows one to draw certain conclusions from probable premises. In this illustration, starting from the two premises that "all fruits can be eaten" and "this apple is a fruit", it can be concluded that "this apple can be eaten".

THE EMPIRE OF ALEXANDER

Frequent warfare brought about crisis in the city-states. The border regions then acquired greater importance. The power of Sparta over the Greek towns was briefly replaced by the power of Thebes and Boetia. In the north, a small kingdom called Macedonia was developing and its destiny was to conquer all of the Greek world and territories far beyond.

Philip II of Macedonia Conquers Greece

From 360 B.C., Philip II, son of Argaeus, ruled over Macedonia. He succeeded in strengthening his kingdom by gathering all the nobles into the court and by reorganizing his army in a more efficient way (the Macedonian phalanx battle formation was a key tactic). Philip intruded in the constant wars between the states, allying with various contenders, and eventually imposed his dominion over Greece. He unified the Greek world but through force, not democracy. Athens resisted, at the urging of Demosthenes, but was defeated. This defeat marked the end of the independence of the Greek cities.

Alexander Conquers the Persian Empire

After Philip's assassination, his son Alexander ascended the throne. He brutally crushed the last attempts of the city-states to regain their independence. He punished Thebes with its total destruction. Then he carried out his father's dream—conquering Persia and creating a vast empire from the Aegean to the Oceanos, the mythical river which the Greeks thought surrounded the earth. In 334 B.C., Alexander launched an attack upon Persia and conquered its empire. He ultimately reached the Indus Valley in India before turning back to Mesopotamia.

The Imperial Design of Alexander

Alexander founded the capital of his empire in Babylon. He believed that he was endowed with a special religious authority, confirmed by Egyptian priests who had proclaimed him the son of god and the successor to the pharaohs. Alexander valued knowledge and

Above: A Macedonian soldier.

The Macedonian infantry, considered invincible, was organized into a phalanx. It was composed of eight thousand infantrymen lined up in sixteen rows.

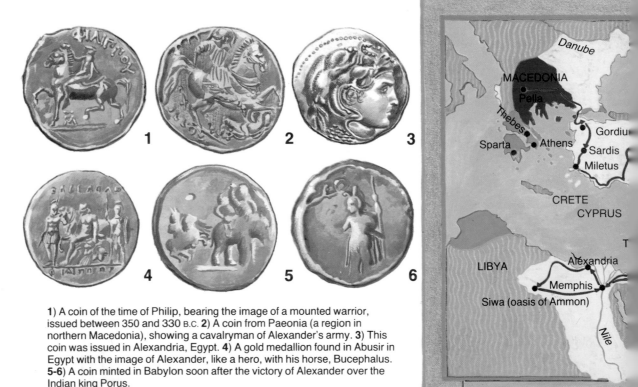

1) A coin of the time of Philip, bearing the image of a mounted warrior, issued between 350 and 330 B.C. 2) A coin from Paeonia (a region in northern Macedonia), showing a cavalryman of Alexander's army. 3) This coin was issued in Alexandria, Egypt. 4) A gold medallion found in Abusir in Egypt with the image of Alexander, like a hero, with his horse, Bucephalus. 5-6) A coin minted in Babylon soon after the victory of Alexander over the Indian king Porus.

This map shows the route of the campaigns of Alexander and the extent of his empire, stretching from Greece to India. Alexander's conquests briefly united Europe and Asia and opened up new communication and trade links.

scientific curiosity, and understood their political value. For this reason, a group of scholars accompanied him on his expeditions. They had the tasks of measuring distances, describing the different countries, and studying the customs and medical practices of the various cultures. He tried to unite the different populations of his empire, and he favoured the union of the East and the West, but this union was never achieved. Ambassadors, as well as Greek, Persian, Celtic, Spanish, Roman and Carthaginian merchants congregated at Alexander's court at Babylon. But the peoples under Alexander's sway remained mutually suspicious, East and West regarding one another as barbarians.

Above: A Persian soldier.

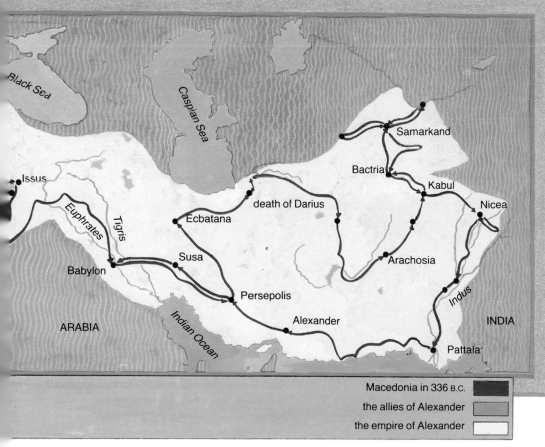

Macedonia in 336 B.C.

the allies of Alexander

the empire of Alexander

In the Greek towns of Asia Minor, the Hellenistic tradition continued, even after the death of Alexander. Shown here is a meeting of members of the boule or council in the council room of the small town of Priene in Ionia.

The Heritage of Alexander

No other general would dominate such a mighty empire, and Alexander's conquests did not long outlive him. On the death of Alexander in 323 B.C., his generals fought each other, then split the empire between them. Three great states emerged: Macedonia, Egypt, and the Middle East.

Hellenistic Monarchy

A Hellenistic monarchy was a form of government in which the powers of the state were in the hands of the king who ruled by the strength of his army. Under the power of the king, the difference between Greek and non-Greek citizens disappeared. An ideal of humanity united through a common allegiance to a sovereign was created. Different peoples could live in political harmony because they found the symbol of their unity and a guarantee for good government in the leadership of their king. The king became a god who was worshipped. After Alexander, the Hellenistic kings were listed among the gods of the Greek towns.

ETRUSCAN ROME AND THE LEGEND OF THE OUSTING OF THE KINGS

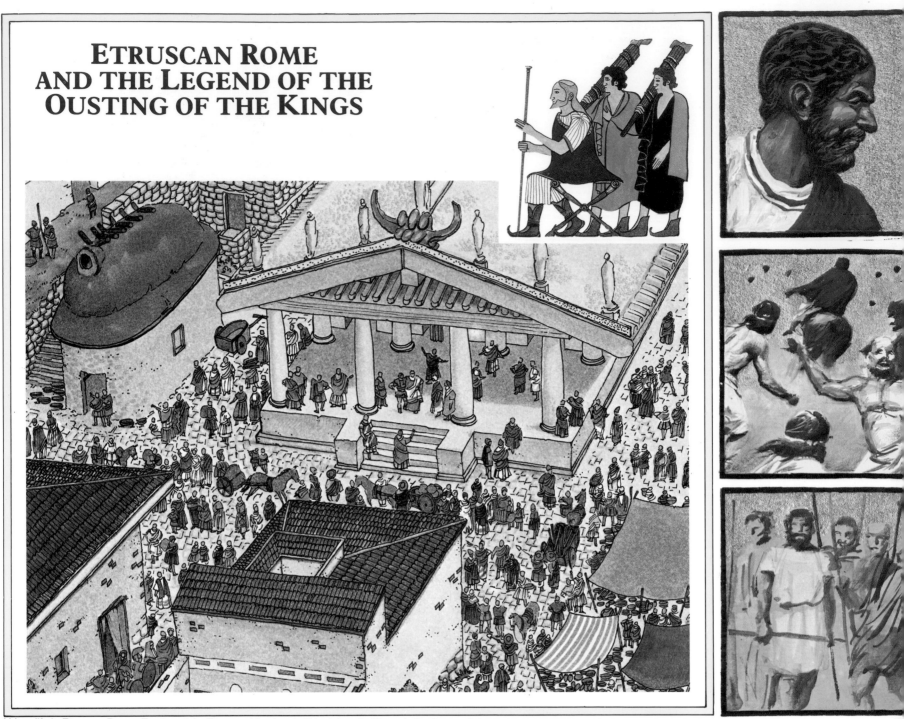

Urban life in Etruscan Rome. *Top insert:* An Etruscan king (seated) is pictured with symbols of power later inherited as Roman symbols: the seat of power and a sceptre. Two officers stand behind the king, holding *fasces*, bundles of rods surrounding an axe which represented authority.

The Civilization of the Etruscans

The Etruscan civilization developed in central Italy. It began around 750 B.C. The Etruscans were descendants of local people and colonists from Asia Minor who had settled there during the early Iron Age. The centre of the Etruscan world was Tuscany, but soon the Etruscans spread beyond the Apennines into the Po Valley and to the south towards the territories of Greater Greece. Skilled sailors and merchants, they were also good at smelting and crafting metals, including iron. The Etruscans were the first to build towns in the regions they inhabited. Their civilization in-

volved a rich religious tradition. The Etruscans believed that the acts of people were sacred, and had to conform to the eternal design of the gods.

Etruscans and Latins in Rome

During their migration southwards, the Etruscans came into contact with the Latin peoples. The Etruscans did not succeed in conquering the region. They had to be satisfied with gaining control of the main trade routes with the rich Greek territories. At points along the River Tiber on several hills, Latin villages had existed for centuries. They eventually unified, forming the nucleus of the city of Rome. Etruscans settled as merchants

in Rome. They later seized power, and it is probable that three Etruscan kings actually ruled the city – Servius Tulius, Tarquinius Priscus, and Tarquinius Superbus, the Proud. The presence of the Etruscans introduced a high degree of civilization into Roman society, which was still basically rural. The population had grown, and there were numerous public buildings. However, there were tensions between the Etruscans and Romans. In the sixth century, opposition against King Tarquinius the Proud grew, and he was ousted. The fall of the king was regarded by Roman historians as the first major event in Rome's rise to power.

SPQR

S.P.Q.R. is the abbreviation for the Latin "Senatus Populusque Romanus," which means "the Senate and people of Rome." This slogan became Rome's watchword. It expressed trust in the Roman people and in Roman institutions.

THE BIRTH OF ROMAN CIVILIZATION

The Roman Republic

Although the Roman people were hostile to Tarquinius and his family, other factors also led to the fall of the king. Around 509 B.C., an Etruscan king, Porsenna of the city of Clusium, invaded Latium, seized Rome, and ousted the family of Tarquinius. Porsenna was based in Rome for his military expeditions throughout Latium, but did not rule the city itself. The Romans, without a king, gave their city an aristocratic government in which most of the political positions were in the hands of the patricians.

The patricians were the most powerful people in Rome. They held the most important magistratures and also had some religious functions.

For a long time, the organization of Rome was similar to that of the Greek city-states. Around the second century B.C., Rome was still an independent and sovereign civic community where city and countryside were tightly bound by common laws. In order to enjoy the full political rights and laws of Rome, a person had to be a citizen.

The Periods of Roman History

The Republican Age (500 B.C.-27 B.C.) started with the ousting of the kings and lasted five centuries. In this period, Rome strengthened its political institutions and its way of life. Roman rule extended throughout Europe and the Mediterranean.

The Imperial Age began with the appointment of the first emperor. The emperors varied greatly in their leadership capabilities and the extent of their power. The early period of the Imperial Age was known as the Principate. In the Principate, the old Republican magistratures were kept intact, and the office of "Princeps" was added. The Princeps was the emperor and the first citizen. He ruled with the collaboration of the senate. Apart from some military conquests, these two centuries were a time of peace. In the later part of the Imperial Age, known as the Dominatus (from A.D. 193 to the time of Constantine, A.D. 324-337), the emperors were almost always elected by the army and ruled without the support of and often in opposition to the senate.

OUR INHERITANCE FROM ROME

Rome was a powerful and often bloodthirsty civilization. Its achievements left permanent marks on Western civilization.

The Pax Deorum

The first Romans inherited from the Etruscans a deep sense of history, a sense of sacredness in which great importance was given to ancestors. People believed that the consequence of good deeds could be inherited, and that errors and faults had to be eliminated. The Romans believed in the existence of a great alliance between the gods and Rome. It was called the Pax Deorum (the peace of the gods). This was the expression of a new trust in the relationship between gods and people, an innovation differing from the Eastern traditions, and even from early Greek philosophy. This belief that the gods supported Rome gave the Romans confidence to embark on overseas enterprises, as they expanded their power throughout the western world. Moreover, it provided the Romans with a great sense of tolerance towards foreigners, and even their enemies. After being conquered, some former foes became "Romanized", and even acquired Roman citizenship. However, others were enslaved or sacrificed in the arena for the amusement of baying crowds. Never tolerated was impiety, public disrespect for the gods of Rome.

Tradition and Innovation

Romans were always conscious of spreading Roman civilization, but in each conquered territory they also tried to absorb the traditions of other cultures. The Romans took advantage of knowledge gained from other peoples to modify their own beliefs and customs.

The Law

In the Greek city-state, written law had marked a huge step forward in civilization. Law in the modern sense was created in Rome. Roman law still remains a model for the legal system of many modern countries.

Europe's Legacy from Rome

When the western Roman Empire started to crumble, lacking internal strength and finally dying, Roman civilization bequeathed a rich legacy to the peoples of Europe. One gift was its legal system, which was to blend with the customs of the various peoples, creating a new governmental and judicial order. Another characteristic was Rome's capacity to assimilate other peoples and cultures. The Pax Deorum was another legacy, expressing belief in an alliance between people and gods.

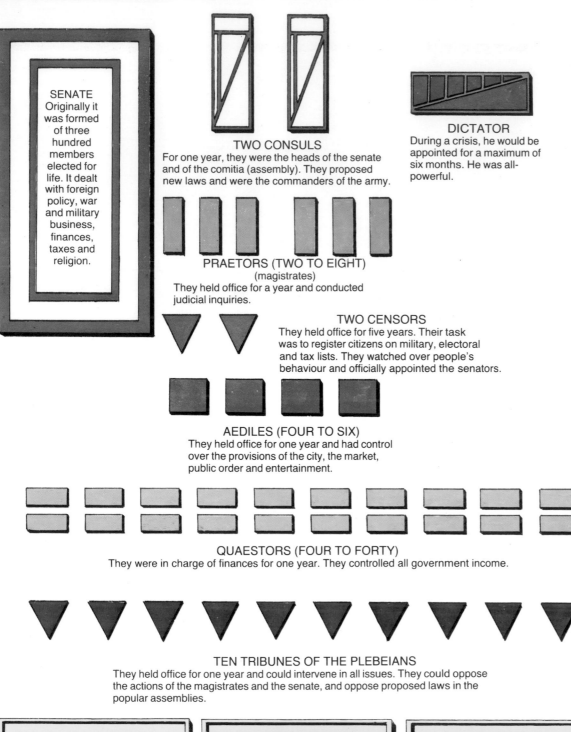

SENATE
Originally it was formed of three hundred members elected for life. It dealt with foreign policy, war and military business, finances, taxes and religion.

TWO CONSULS
For one year, they were the heads of the senate and of the comitia (assembly). They proposed new laws and were the commanders of the army.

DICTATOR
During a crisis, he would be appointed for a maximum of six months. He was all-powerful.

PRAETORS (TWO TO EIGHT)
(magistrates)
They held office for a year and conducted judicial inquiries.

TWO CENSORS
They held office for five years. Their task was to register citizens on military, electoral and tax lists. They watched over people's behaviour and officially appointed the senators.

AEDILES (FOUR TO SIX)
They held office for one year and had control over the provisions of the city, the market, public order and entertainment.

QUAESTORS (FOUR TO FORTY)
They were in charge of finances for one year. They controlled all government income.

TEN TRIBUNES OF THE PLEBEIANS
They held office for one year and could intervene in all issues. They could oppose the actions of the magistrates and the senate, and oppose proposed laws in the popular assemblies.

Comitia Curiata	**Comitia Centuriata**	**Comitia Tributa**
Originally, this was an assembly of shepherds and farmers. It retained its importance at all times and had the task of appointing the magistrates.	The participants were divided into classes according to their wealth, and each class was divided into centuries (groups), just like the army. They elected the consuls, the censors and the praetors; decided upon peace or war; and judged trials which involved capital punishment for Roman citizens.	The citizens of this assembly were divided into thirty-five rural and urban districts (called tribes) according to the place where they lived. Both patricians and plebeians had a right to vote. The assembly would elect aediles and quaestors, examine the body of laws, and act in judgement during trials of certain crimes.

PEOPLE'S ASSEMBLY
Everybody could participate in this assembly, but it was mainly attended by plebeians. The assembly elected the tribunes of the plebeians and the plebeian aediles. It would also vote on the laws, called plebiscites, proposed by the tribunes.

SOCIETY AND INSTITUTIONS IN REPUBLICAN ROME

Patricians, Nobles and Knights

The patricians embodied Rome's political and religious establishment. Besides them, another group of powerful people, the nobles, developed in Rome. They were the descendants of people who had held the most important magistratures. As a public position was usually passed from father to son, the nobles came to control the main magistratures in Rome.

The nobles were very wealthy. Their wealth was based on land. Life as a land-owner was considered the most dignified way of existence. Also very wealthy were the knights, who became numerous around the end of the Republican Age. They were plebeians (commoners) who had become rich and thus could hold public office. They could abandon activities considered undignified, such as commerce, and achieve a status comparable to that of the nobles. Eventually, they could join the noble class. All three classes – patricians, nobles and knights – numbered no more than a few thousand people.

The Plebeians

The class of Roman plebeians may have originated from conquered peoples who migrated to Rome. In the Republican Age, the plebeians were not a homogenous group. They included poor peasants, who lived by their labour, and artisans and merchants, who were in a better position financially. In spite of these social and economic differences, the plebeians were considered a single class by the state.

The Slaves

Like other civilizations in the ancient world, but on a far greater scale, the Romans had slaves. Slaves were people without rights who could be bought. In Rome, slaves were often prisoners of war or people who had fallen into debt. Slaves worked in the mines, in the fields, on vast estates or in specialized farming. Sometimes they would be installed as tenant farmers. In the city, domestic slaves worked as servants in homes. Some took care of the finances and helped their masters in artisan or trade activities. Occasionally a slave would be released from servitude and obtain Roman citizenship.

The chart shows administrative units of the Roman Republic.

The Client Relationship Between Rich and Poor

Patricians and nobles each had their "clients" among the plebeians. They had the duty of welcoming the clients in their houses, feeding them when necessary, protecting and helping them. In turn, the clients had to pay homage to the patrician or noble, and back him in any public or private issue. The clients enjoyed the protection of their patron, which was indispensable in political, legal and economic life. The powerful, on the other hand, were all the more influential if they had a lot of clients.

The Senate and the Comitia in Rome

Over the centuries, the Roman public structure developed along with the growth of the city. Eventually a unit made of numerous magistratures and assemblies was created. The organization of power was based on the senate and on the people. In the Republican Age, the senate became the main political instrument. It dealt with foreign policy and war, checked finances and taxes, watched over religious life and supervised military affairs. The people expressed their wishes through comitia or assemblies. These assemblies had political weight, provided they met in accordance with the law. The comitia served the purpose of voting on the laws, handing down verdicts and choosing the magistrates. The patricians and nobles controlled political life in Rome because they held the most important magistratures and because they organized voting procedures within the assembly.

The Plebeians Against Patricians and Nobles

Since the very beginning of the Republican Age, the plebeians, mainly the wealthiest among them, had claimed the right to take part in political decisions. In 494 B.C., the plebeians threatened to break the agreement which permitted the existence of the republic. They withdrew from the sacred enclosure of the city. They returned to Rome only when they obtained their own tribunes, an assembly of plebeians, and aediles of their choosing.

The Comitia Centuriata was the most important assembly of the Roman people. It met outside the walls of the city because it represented the military armed for battle, which could not enter the sacred enclosure of the city. A special enclosed space was organized for the gathering on the "Field of Mars" (parade grounds). The assembly was informed of the issues to be decided, and then a vote was taken. In the beginning, the vote was oral. Each individual was questioned by an officer, and the answer was entered into a register. In the first century B.C., the secret, written ballot was introduced.

Below: The composition of Roman society.

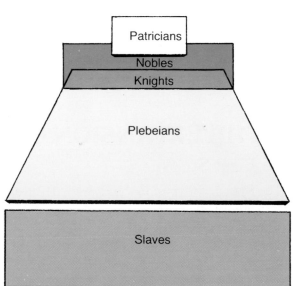

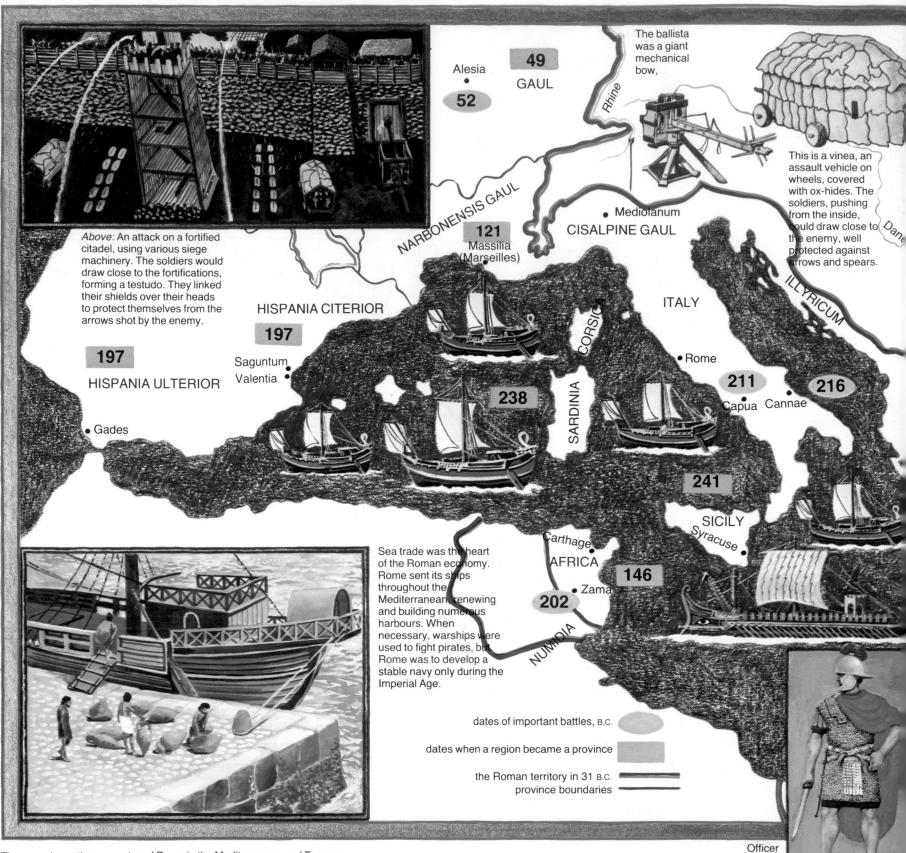

The ballista was a giant mechanical bow,

This is a vinea, an assault vehicle on wheels, covered with ox-hides. The soldiers, pushing from the inside, could draw close to the enemy, well protected against arrows and spears.

Above: An attack on a fortified citadel, using various siege machinery. The soldiers would draw close to the fortifications, forming a testudo. They linked their shields over their heads to protect themselves from the arrows shot by the enemy.

49
Alesia
GAUL
52

121
Massilia (Marseilles)

NARBONENSIS GAUL

Mediolanum
CISALPINE GAUL

ITALY

ILLYRICUM

HISPANIA CITERIOR
197

CORSICA

Rome

211

216

HISPANIA ULTERIOR
197

Saguntum
Valentia

238

SARDINIA

Capua Cannae

Gades

241

SICILY
Syracuse

Sea trade was the heart of the Roman economy. Rome sent its ships throughout the Mediterranean, renewing and building numerous harbours. When necessary, warships were used to fight pirates, but Rome was to develop a stable navy only during the Imperial Age.

Carthage
AFRICA

Zama

146

202

NUMIDIA

dates of important battles, B.C.

dates when a region became a province

the Roman territory in 31 B.C.
province boundaries

The map shows the expansion of Rome in the Mediterranean and Europe.

Officer

THE EXPANSION OF REPUBLICAN ROME

The First Steps

The Romans believed that they were destined by the gods to conquer others. They demonstrated great skill in fostering the coexistence of diverse conquered peoples. The young republic took its first steps in Italy against the Etruscan towns of the north, against Latin neighbours, and against Greek towns in the south.

The Punic Wars

The Romans clashed with the Carthaginians in three wars for dominance of the western half of the Mediterranean. As a result of the First Punic War (264-238 B.C.), the Romans gained Sardinia and Corsica. In the Second Punic War (221-202 B.C.), in spite of the victories of the Carthaginian general Hannibal

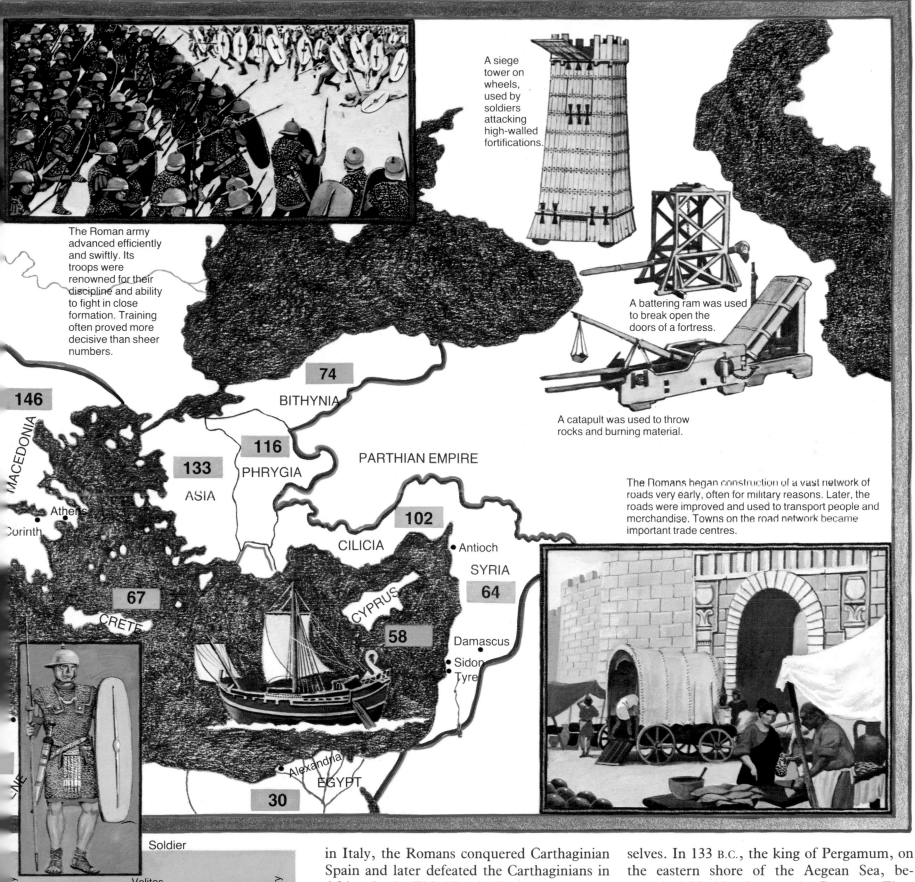

The Roman army advanced efficiently and swiftly. Its troops were renowned for their discipline and ability to fight in close formation. Training often proved more decisive than sheer numbers.

A siege tower on wheels, used by soldiers attacking high-walled fortifications.

A battering ram was used to break open the doors of a fortress.

A catapult was used to throw rocks and burning material.

The Romans began construction of a vast network of roads very early, often for military reasons. Later, the roads were improved and used to transport people and merchandise. Towns on the road network became important trade centres.

146

MACEDONIA

74

BITHYNIA

116

133

PHRYGIA

ASIA

PARTHIAN EMPIRE

Athens

Corinth

102

CILICIA

Antioch

SYRIA

64

CYPRUS

67

CRETE

58

Damascus

Sidon

Tyre

Alexandria

EGYPT

30

Soldier

Cavalry

Velites

Cavalry

Javelin Throwers

Principes

Triarii

The second line was made up of heavy infantry, the principes. In the third line were the veterans, or triarii. The cavalry operated on the flanks.

in Italy, the Romans conquered Carthaginian Spain and later defeated the Carthaginians in Africa. In the Third Punic War (149-146 B.C.), the politicians who were in favour of expansion and colonization obtained a majority in Rome. As a result, Carthage was destroyed, and a Roman province in Africa was founded.

The Conquest of the East

At first, the Romans defended the independence of the Greek city-states against the Hellenistic sovereigns. But later, in 148 B.C., Rome conquered Greece and Macedonia them-

selves. In 133 B.C., the king of Pergamum, on the eastern shore of the Aegean Sea, bequeathed his kingdom to the Romans. They turned Pergamum into a new province called Asia.

The Organization of Roman Provinces

In order to rule over peoples with different cultures and political traditions, the Romans created new administrative units ruled by a Roman magistrate. The people of these provinces were not granted Roman citizenship.

Celtic iron tools, many of which have altered little in design in two thousand years.

THE GAULS AND THE CELTIC WORLD

During the first centuries of the Roman republic, numerous tribes of Celtic peoples had spread throughout the vast stretch of territory of temperate Europe, from the Atlantic Ocean to the Black Sea. These peoples had created a civilization with a common language, culture and religion. The Celts settled in the British Isles, arriving in a series of migrations from mainland Europe.

The First Celtic Towns

The Gauls, skilled farmers, had long been living in small villages, scattered about in the countryside. They had not merged into more complex settlements. Around the third century B.C., however, the tribes which lived in Cisalpine Gaul (now northern Italy) began to build fortified settlements of a primitive type, known by the Latin term *oppidum*. By the second century, several such towns existed in France, Germany, Bohemia and Hungary.

Town Life Reaches Northern Europe

The Celtic *oppidae* were the first towns to

appear in Europe north of the Mediterranean region, which had already had urban civilizations for a considerable time. The oppidae were large in area, enclosed within sturdy defensive walls. The space within the walls was left partially free of buildings and was used as a shelter for cattle as well as for farmers in time of danger. The towns possessed temples, aristocratic dwellings, homes and artisan workshops.

Defensive Fortifications

The existence of these towns reflected growing economic prosperity, but also military uncertainty. Each town probably had a defensive role. The walls were built of stone and

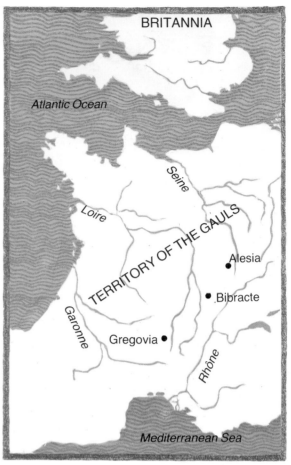

A map showing the territory of the Gauls, covering much of today's France, with the sites of three important oppidae.

A typical Celtic settlement, or oppidum. The quarters for the artisans were located along the defensive walls, built using the "Gallic walls" technique. Outside the town walls, wheat was harvested. The farmland was a balance of woods, fields and pastures. A priest, or druid, is shown returning from the woods having gathered some magical herbs.

wood. These Celtic craftsmen also worked with ceramics, glass and enamels. Their great ability in working iron permitted them to manufacture all the tools they needed for a range of jobs. Tools of similar shape were found throughout Celtic Europe. This suggests that the basic manufacturing techniques were known and used throughout the areas inhabited by Celts.

The Flourishing Countryside

The change which occurred in the countryside was less radical. The Celts had already developed cultivation methods which made the best use of the typical climatic and soil features of temperate Europe. Their farming created the typical European landscape, where ploughed fields and woods alternated with pastures for grazing animals. The improvement of artisan skills, however, gave agriculture more efficient iron tools, first and foremost the plough. The flourishing of agriculture made some Celtic regions, especially Gaul, particularly wealthy. These regions became more densely populated than others.

timber in a style which the Roman emperor Julius Caesar called "Gallic walls". The walls reflected the influence of Mediterranean building techniques. These techniques were perhaps brought north of the Alps by Celts from the Mediterranean regions. The fortified towns were a defensive reaction to the hostile presence of German tribes and, to the east along the River Danube, the Dacians.

Skilled Celtic Artisans

Specialized artisans formed the nucleus of the Celts living in the oppidae. Their technical skills were outstanding. They were superb wagon-makers. They invented the barrel, combining skills in the working of iron and

North-central Europe, showing the territory of the Germans.

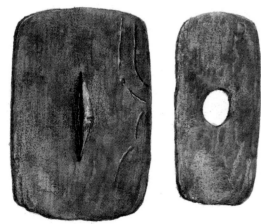

Wooden shields found in a swamp in Denmark, dating back to around 100 B.C.

THE GERMANS

At the end of the second century B.C., new tribes of Germanic stock came into contact with the Roman and Celtic peoples.

The Germans were a people composed of numerous tribes. They originated in the northern part of the European plain, in Denmark and the Scandinavian peninsula.

Celts and Germans

To the west and south, the Germanic territory bordered on Celtic territory. The two peoples had previously established trade links, but the situation changed when the German tribes started to move towards the more desirable lands of central and southern Europe. The Celts were more urbanized than the Germans. They had cavalry, possibly organized into a permanent army. The strategies and fighting techniques of the two peoples were vastly different. Each Celt carried a long sword, a spear, and a shield. Celts wore helmets and were fond of attacking in formation. The Germans had a highly mobile light cavalry. Their tactics were to draw close, launch an attack and retreat.

The First Military Clash Between Celts and Romans

The Celtic people were no longer expanding. They had been defeated by the Romans, first in Italy and later in Provence, in southern France. There, in 125 B.C., the Romans founded the province of Narbonne Gaul.

Around 120 B.C., a Germanic tribe from Denmark, the Cimbri, clashed with the most powerful Celtic tribe of central Europe, the Boii, who ruled Bavaria. Following the amber trade route, the Cimbri moved south and defeated the Romans in Styria (Austria). They did not march on Italy but, within a few years, reached southern Gaul, along with other tribes of German and Celtic origin. The invaders stormed the region until they were defeated by the Romans in 102 B.C. at Aix-en-Provence and in 101 B.C. at Vercelli in the Po Valley.

Pressure from the German tribes continued, and several groups established settlements west of the Rhine in northern Gaul. Around 70 B.C.,

Typical hairstyle of a German, reconstructed on the evidence of skull remains.

Artist's impression of houses in the German colony of Ezinge in Holland, dating from the third century B.C.

A votive bronze necklace in the shape of a crown from lower Saxony, Germany, third century B.C.

A vase found in a cremation grave in Denmark, dating back to the first century B.C.

Visualization of a cavalry clash between Gauls and Germans near Admagetobriga in the Alsace region. The Germans, led by Ariovistus, defeated the Gallic cavalry and settled on the lands of the Sequani Gauls. *Left inset:* a Gallic cavalryman. *Right inset:* a German cavalryman.

the greatest pressure point was probably the region north of the River Main. The German leader Ariovistus, who lived in this region, was recruited with his army by the Sequani Gauls, who needed help in the battle against their arch rivals, the Aedui. In exchange for his services, Ariovistus obtained permission to settle in their territory, modern Alsace. On the arrival of the Germans the Sequani were seized by panic. They tried to resist but were defeated at Admagetobriga on the Alsatian side of the Rhine. The domination of the Germans was so harsh that after a few years the Gauls asked for help from the Romans. The Romans, led by Julius Caesar, defeated Ariovistus near Besançon in 58 B.C.

Caesar's plan was to establish the boundary of German territory along the banks of the Rhine. Then he could control the territory of Gaul, which he was preparing to conquer. This plan was followed by all later Roman leaders, except for occasional raids on the far side of the Rhine. Neither the Gauls nor the Romans, however, succeeded in pushing the Germans back from the Rhine. Nor could they prevent other tribes from gradually infiltrating across the border and settling in Gaul.

German Pressure Grows

The arrival of this new German foe caused serious problems for the Celts. In the same year as the defeat of Ariovistus, 58 B.C., the Helvetians made an unsuccessful attempt to migrate west from their land in western Switzerland. They were stopped by other tribes and by the Romans, and forced to return to the regions they had abandoned. Their population was reduced by almost half. At the end of the first century B.C., the German tribe of Marcomanni, led by Maroboduus, reached the territory of the Boians in central Europe. The Quadi tribe invaded what is now Moravia, further east. The Celtic culture in these territories was crushed within a short time. Numerous settlements were destroyed, some of the Celtic population fled, the rest became subject to the Germanic newcomers.

Pompey (106-48 B.C.)

Marius (155-86 B.C.)

Sulla (138-78 B.C.)

Crassus (115-53 B.C.)

Julius Caesar
(100-44 B.C.)

In the first decades of the first century B.C., a major economic crisis swept Rome, causing a number of riots. This drawing shows a mob looting a bakery.

THE CRISIS OF THE REPUBLIC AND JULIUS CAESAR

New Farming Policies, New Estates

The early Roman economy was based on raising livestock and farming small plots. The land was worked by the entire family with the help of a few slaves. When such small landowners had to serve as soldiers in the many battles fought by Rome, they sometimes had to abandon their land. The importation of cheap wheat from the provinces caused the decline of the traditional Italian grain cultivation. Wealthy landowners introduced vineyards, olive groves, vegetables and fruit trees. These new crops often required intensive labour and heavy expense. The small farmers had to sell their plots. This reduced the number of free landowners. Senators and aristocrats who had both political power and economic means could take advantage of the land seizures and create larger estates.

Rome's Wealth Increases

Great riches in currency and gold, principally the booty of war, began to flow into Rome. The systematic exploitation of the provinces provided large quantities of money both to the state and to private enterprises. The population of Rome increased greatly, partly because of migration of poor people from the countryside. Urban development and public works multiplied the opportunities for work and circulated the great wealth. In 269 B.C., Rome started to mint silver coins.

Political and Social Struggles

Starting in the second half of the second century, these economic changes caused several kinds of political and social crises. Nobles, plebeians and slaves were at odds. There were attempts to take illegally held grazing land away from the great livestock farmers and to divide the land among the citizens. In 104-102 B.C., the slaves of Campania and Sicily rebelled. In 72-71 B.C., an ex-slave named Spartacus led a rebellion of slaves. The uprising was harshly repressed. In 91 B.C., the Italic confederation started a war which was concluded with their attainment of citizenship in 89 B.C.

An economic crisis hit Rome. The city was overcrowded with refugees, provisions were scarce, and prices were rising rapidly. Riots broke out. There were two opposing factions. The senate and the nobles wished their power and privilege to remain unchanged. The wealthy plebeians, called populares, wanted to seize political power equal to their economic power, and they wanted decisive action in foreign affairs including new overseas colonies. Marius was the leader of the popular movement, while Sulla was backed by most of the nobles and the wealthiest classes. Sulla

A reconstruction of the Celtic settlement of Bigbury in England. Caesar found such Celtic walled towns during his raid in 55 B.C.

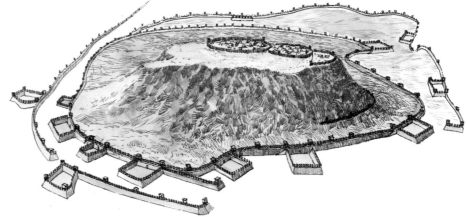

The site of the Battle of Alesia. On top of the hill there was a fortified Gallic oppidum surrounded by a double line of siege fortifications which the Romans had built to cut off supplies.

Roman soldiers confiscate lands in a Gallic village they have just conquered and drive away the former inhabitants.

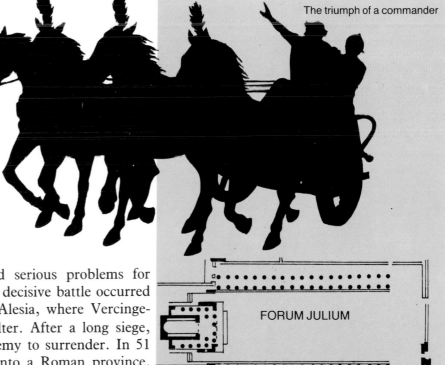

The triumph of a commander

prevailed and for three years violently imposed his dictatorship on Rome.

The Rise of Julius Caesar

Several years of internal conflict followed. Among the most famous struggles for power and the ensuing conspiracies was the conspiracy of Catiline.

Julius Caesar, a member of a noble Roman family, took part in the conspiracy and sided with Catiline against the aristocratic proconsul Cicero. When the conspiracy failed, Caesar left Rome for some years. In 60 B.C., he returned and founded an informal alliance, the first triumvirate. He became ruler of Cisalpine Gaul and Narbonensis Gaul for five years. In 58 B.C., Caesar went to the provinces that had been assigned to him and began the conquest of the rest of the Gallic lands. He clashed with the courageous king Vercingetorix of the Arverni, who created serious problems for Caesar's legions. The decisive battle occurred around the town of Alesia, where Vercingetorix had sought shelter. After a long siege, Caesar forced the enemy to surrender. In 51 B.C., he made Gaul into a Roman province. Thanks to the victories in Gaul, Caesar could return to Rome victorious and impose his will on the senate. After defeating his rival Pompey, he gained indisputable political power over the Roman state.

Towards Empire

With the rise of Julius Caesar, the concept of a single ruler started to take hold in Rome. In 44 B.C., Caesar was assassinated. About sixty senators, the last defenders of the republic, took part in the conspiracy.

The Forum of Julius Caesar

The forum in Rome was a central square surrounded by temples, public buildings, colonnades and commercial buildings with statues, inscriptions, and commemorative columns. It was the financial, religious and administrative centre of the city. Julius Caesar also created a new square with a temple dedicated to Venus Genetrix to give thanks for the victory over his rival, Pompey.

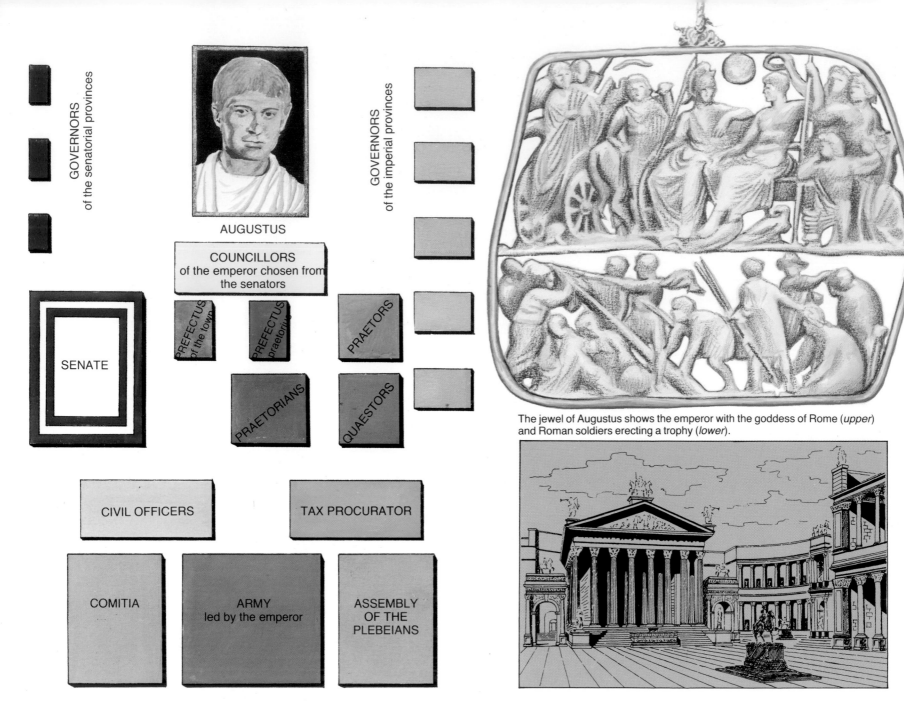

GOVERNORS of the senatorial provinces

AUGUSTUS

GOVERNORS of the imperial provinces

COUNCILLORS of the emperor chosen from the senators

PREFECTUS of the town

PREFECTUS praetorius

PRAETORS

SENATE

PRAETORIANS

QUAESTORS

CIVIL OFFICERS

TAX PROCURATOR

COMITIA

ARMY led by the emperor

ASSEMBLY OF THE PLEBEIANS

As *Princeps*, Augustus held the powers of an emperor, at the centre of Rome's political administration.

The jewel of Augustus shows the emperor with the goddess of Rome (*upper*) and Roman soldiers erecting a trophy (*lower*).

The forum built by Augustus, with the temple dedicated to Mars the Avenger.

THE BIRTH OF THE EMPIRE:
THE PRINCIPATE OF OCTAVIAN

The Rise of Octavian

After the death of Caesar, the struggle for power in Rome resumed. A second triumvirate was created. Each of the three rulers had a sphere of influence. Octavian ruled over the west, Lepidus ruled over Africa and Mark Antony ruled over the east. But this division of power was not to last long, and soon Octavian made his bid to gain sole control of the Roman state. He violently expelled the senate and the friends of Antony. In 31 B.C., in the battle of Actium, he defeated Antony's fleet, which was backed by the Egyptian fleet of Cleopatra. Lepidus had already retired from political life. So after the defeat of Antony, Octavian became the empire's uncontested ruler.

The Principate

Octavian considered himself the supreme defender of Rome and its traditions, in contrast to the despotism of the eastern monarchies. After his victory, he devised an original way of imposing his power, while preserving the traditional political institutions. This new government was called a Principate. Octavian laid the foundation for the Principate through collaboration with the major powers of Roman society. He did not embark upon sudden and major reform of the political institutions. Instead he changed them gradually, continually concentrating more power in his own hands. He respected the authority of the senate and so did not alter its constitution, rather appointing

himself president of the senate. He took the power once held by several officials, such as the tribunes of the plebeians, for himself, and kept the power permanently, rather than for one year. His authority, his moral influence, his personal dignity, and his military expertise made him overwhelmingly superior to anyone else. In 27 B.C., in recognition of his authority, Octavian was given the title of "Augustus", which acknowledged his personal prestige and the fact that he was protected by the gods. Later, in 12 B.C., Augustus was appointed *pontifex maximus*, head of the Roman priesthood.

Augustus divided the provinces into two groups – imperial and senatorial. The former was directly administered by him through

The Roman army attacking an Alpine fortification. The conquest of the Alps and the creation of new provinces in these regions was one of the main successes of Augustus. *Left:* The giant monument of the Turbie, built in Provence in 7-6 B.C. It honoured the conquest of the Alpine tribes between 16 and 14 B.C.

trusted legates, while the latter was under the control of the senate. Taxes from the senate-controlled provinces were collected in the treasury of the state. Taxes from the imperial provinces were collected in the treasury of the emperor, for his personal benefit. The new organization of the provinces provided some relief for local populations from the abuse of power that had occurred during the Republican Age. Moreover, they could appeal directly to the emperor in case of discontent.

Military Campaigns

The principal aims of Augustus were the pacification of the lands annexed to the empire, and the creation of secure frontiers. His main concern was to conquer the Alpine tribes, who still retained their independence. He succeeded in imposing Roman domination and creating new provinces. To the north, the Romans invaded German territories, but were halted on the River Elbe and driven back by the Germans under the leadership of the chief of the Cherusci, Arminius, who had served in the Roman army. The crucial battle was fought in the Teutoberg forest in A.D. 9. Three Roman legions were wiped out. The Roman border was consolidated along the Rhine. In the east, Augustus had to give up his plan of imposing military domination over the Parthians and Armenians.

THE ROMAN RELIGION

The Roman Gods

The group of gods worshipped by Roman people originally consisted of a triad of deities – Jupiter, the god who had supreme sovereignty; Mars, the god of war; and Quirinus, the god of the city. During the period of the Roman monarchy, due to the influence of the Etruscans, great importance had been given to Juno and Minerva. Juno was the wife of Jupiter and the goddess of fertility; Minerva was the protector of all professions.

The Alliance with the Gods

The Romans believed in the Pax Deorum (peace with the gods) and considered this alliance an absolute necessity. It was an alliance between the gods and all Roman citizens. The belief was that Rome would endure so long as the gods were on its side. The Greeks felt helpless in the face of death, which put an end to all personal creation and development. The Romans, on the other hand, forged a connection between the dead and the living through a sense of great unity with their ancestors.

Priests

The numerous groups of priests had the task of celebrating the rituals of the main deities. The principal holders of the sacred sciences were called the pontifices. They knew the calendar, the most suitable invocations and prayers, and the rules that regulated the various temples. They formed a college led by the pontifex maximus. In Rome, special importance was given to Vesta, the goddess who guaranteed the continued existence of the city. A perpetual flame burned in the middle of a small round temple dedicated to Vesta. Should the flame go out, Rome would be destroyed. Special priestesses, vowed to celibacy and known as the Vestal Virgins, dedicated their lives to the goddess and the preservation of the sacred flame.

Family Pietas and the Domestic Cult

At the root of Roman religion was the life of each home and family. Obedience to one's father, called family *pietas* (piety), was the foundation of Roman civilization.

Precise rituals accompanied the major stages in a Roman's life – birth, adolescence, marriage and death. Marriage, for example, took place under the protection of Juno and of the household deities. In ancient times, there was

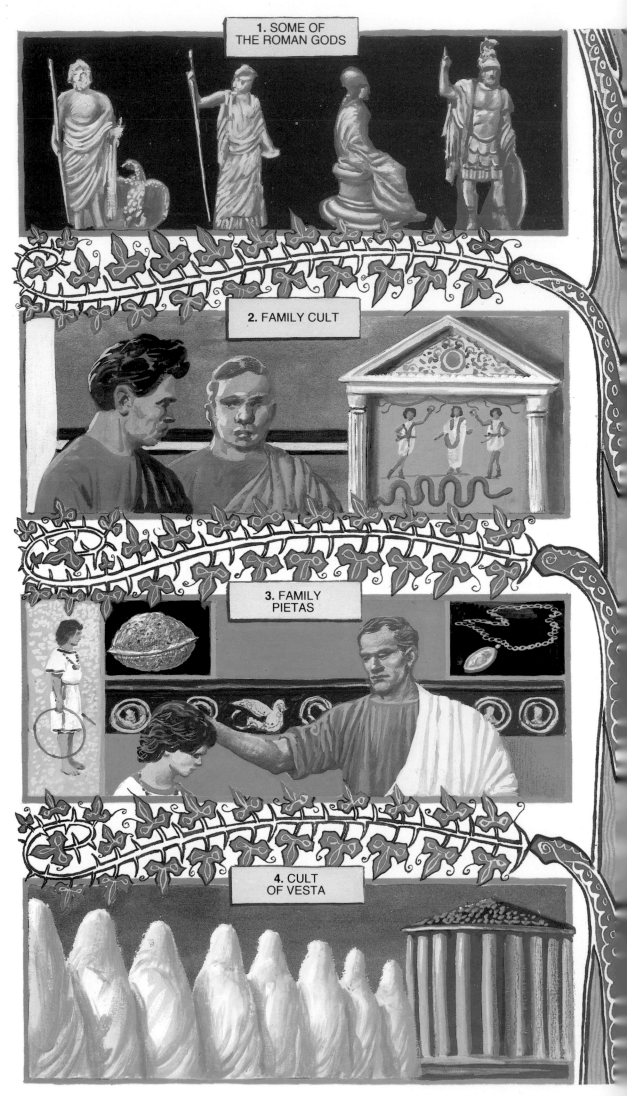

1. SOME OF THE ROMAN GODS

2. FAMILY CULT

3. FAMILY PIETAS

4. CULT OF VESTA

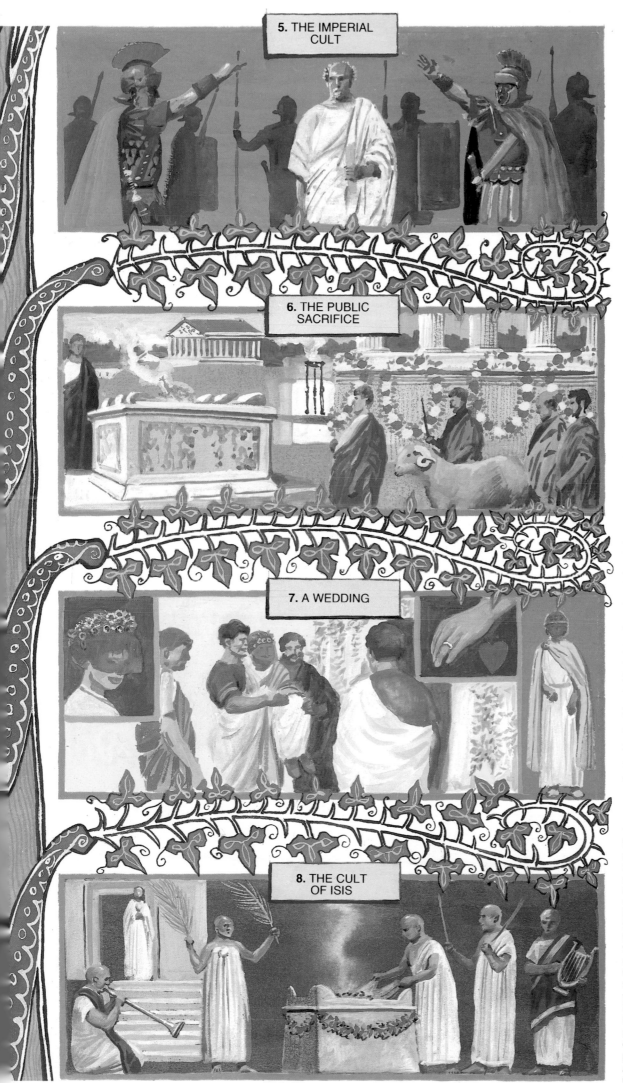

5. THE IMPERIAL CULT

6. THE PUBLIC SACRIFICE

7. A WEDDING

8. THE CULT OF ISIS

always a fire burning at the centre of the house, later replaced by an altar located in the communal room. Among the offerings were flower garlands, incense, wine, honey and sweets.

The Cult of the Emperor

Augustus had given Rome peace, freeing it from the threat of internal strife and consolidating Roman power in the world. So it was not difficult for the Romans to consider such a man to be divine. The divinity of Augustus was honoured both in Rome and in the provinces. After his reign, the deification of all emperors became the rule. The senate had the task of declaring the divinity of the emperor after his death, and all the inhabitants of the empire were expected to celebrate the imperial cult. Any group who did not follow this rule was accused of endangering the solidity of the empire itself.

Religious Influences from the East

After the Punic Wars and during the internal unrest of the Republican Age, the Romans started to lose faith in their alliance with the gods, who did not seem to provide answers to the doubts and sufferings of people. The concept of a relationship between human beings and their destiny was starting to develop. No longer did the destiny of Rome itself influence religious ideas. Newer, more personal creeds appeared, for the great power of Rome was no longer sufficient in itself to give meaning to human existence. New explanations were sought in eastern religions. In the first century B.C., the cult of Isis was introduced from Egypt. In this cult, a few chosen individuals would perform rituals which represented a person's death and resurrection.

1) Jupiter, Juno, Minerva and Mars. 2) In the atrium of the house, in front of the altar of the Lares (house gods), the head of the family prepares to celebrate a ritual. 3) A son had to obey his father completely in accordance with ancient tradition. The walnut was the symbol of youth as was the bulla, an amulet, which youths wore around their necks until they were seventeen years of age. 4) Priestesses going to the temple of Vesta, where the eternal flame, representing the goddess, burns. 5) The praetorians pay homage to the imperial deity, saluting the emperor with arms outstretched. 6) In front of each temple was an altar where sacrifices to the gods were made. 7) The wedding celebration was rich in symbols. The bride wore a special dress and a veil. When she reached the house of the groom, she might not touch the threshold but was carried across it by her friends. She wore a ring on her ring finger, which according to the Romans contained a nerve that ran all the way to the heart. 8) A priest celebrates a sacrifice on an Egyptian-style altar. Another priest descends the staircase, bearing a holy urn, possibly containing water from the Nile.

DAILY LIFE IN IMPERIAL ROME

An Imperial Capital

In the first century A.D. Rome was changing. It was no longer the city of the early Republican Age, where the people lived like the herdsmen and farmers of the countryside. The city was powerful. It was the meeting place for people from distant provinces, and a great deal of wealth circulated there. Its population was large. At the time of Augustus it reached about one million.

Life in Rome offered the best and the worst of urban experience in ancient times. On the one hand, it allowed for communication between people and the exchange of customs, varied languages and religions. On the other hand, most Romans had no stable source of income. The mob was fond of violent entertainment such as gladiatorial contests where men fought to the death.

Roman High-Rise

To house an increasingly large population, the Romans devised a new kind of housing, the *insula*. This was a high-rise building made up of several apartments similar to a modern block of flats. Usually there were shops on the ground floor. The blocks were often as tall as five or six storeys, and soon became the most popular kind of housing in the city. Buildings of this kind were found both in Rome and Ostia, a densely populated harbour town at the mouth of the River Tiber. The city of Rome did not have distinct rich and poor districts. Most classes lived side by side, with the town homes of the wealthy beside the insulae of the less well-off.

On the right is an aerial view of the Trajan market, a large commercial centre with shops on several levels. This complex was part of the new grandiose forum which the emperor Trajan erected beside the forum of Augustus in the heart of Rome.

Below: This is how the shops along a Roman street looked. Shown are a blacksmith's shop, a poultry shop, a money lender, a grocery store, and a shop selling take-away food. In the background is an insula, a typical apartment building with several storeys.

How the Rich Lived in Town and Country

In the city, rich aristocrats lived with their families in a *domus*, a large private house. The house was spacious and its rooms and courtyard were richly appointed with furniture, statues and frescos.

Most rich people owned several *villas* in the country. These were large farmhouses located in the middle of the estate. At the villa labour was organized, cattle took shelter, and produce could be stored and processed. Part of the building was used as a dwelling by the

Quality control—an inspector checks the finish of some jars.

owner, who lived there from time to time. The farming activities were under the direction of an administrator who organized the labour of the numerous slaves. These types of villas were to become widespread throughout the countryside.

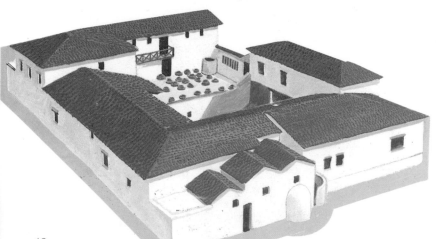

Reconstruction of a villa at Boscoreale in southern Italy. In the second inner courtyard are jars partially buried in the ground, and used to store grain or oil.

The rooms of the Domus.
1. Entrance or "fauces"
2. Atrium, originally the site of the eternal flame and later the central part of the public section of the house
3. Servant's room
4. Office of owner or of his steward
5. Living room or "tablinium"
6. Hallway
7. Bathroom

Inside the atrium of an aristocrat's domus, three clients wait for the owner to appear. In the kitchen (9), a slave is working, and in the weaving room (17), another slave is unrolling a carpet which she has taken off the loom.

8. Inner courtyard with garden
9. Kitchen
10. Storage room
11. Oven
12. Hot bath
13. Warm bath
14. Changing room
15. Summer dining room
16. Bedroom
17. Weaving room
18. The library and main dining room are in this part of the atrium

A noble sits to have a marble bust sculpted. The cabinet in the background contains the busts of his ancestors. These were carried in procession on the occasion of the funeral of a family member, and the right to own and display them was a privilege reserved for the noble class. The nobility of the family was measured by the number of such busts which were kept in the domus.

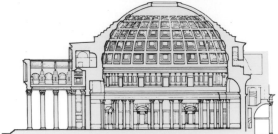

A cross-section of the Pantheon, a temple built by Hadrian in A.D. 126. It is composed of a portico connected to a circular room which is covered by a large, superbly designed dome.

Below: Frieze from Trajan's Column depicting the emperor attacking barbarians.

Below is another frieze from Trajan's Column showing the triumph of the emperor, while defeated enemies beg for mercy.

Poetry readings were held in the library of Maecenas in Rome.

Middle left: Trajan's Column was erected in Rome by Trajan in A.D. 113 to celebrate his conquests. It is decorated with a magnificent marble frieze which winds all the way from the base to the top.

THE POET VIRGIL

LAW, ART AND LITERATURE OF THE EMPIRE

Law and a Legal System Develop in Rome

The Romans were a very law-minded people, and were foremost in creating a legal system that still influences our laws today. In the beginning, Roman law was composed of religious rituals and of rules handed down, and which only applied to Roman-born individuals. However, as the republic expanded, new regulations were introduced which were also applicable to non-native Romans. The Roman lawmakers then began to elaborate on the idea of a system of justice which was uniform for all people, regardless of differences in citizenship, class or wealth. In the first century B.C., the Romans proclaimed the existence of a natural law which stated that all people were equal. This concept was voiced by Cicero, a famous lawmaker and politician. In essence, it meant that the law of the state was only partially the result of laws made by assemblies. The judicial process (the courts) could refine and define laws, and controversial issues could be solved following the principles of natural justice and equity. State law was above everything, and the magistrates drew their authority from it. According to Cicero, in order to be free, an individual had to obey the law.

Literature and Poetry

In the reign of Augustus, the arts flourished in Rome. Many poets and writers would gather in the city house or country villa of Maecenas, a diplomat and counsellor to Augustus. The emperor himself followed these artistic activities, which were supposed to celebrate the peace and power of Rome. Among the writers in this circle were Horace,

Two examples of Roman
triumphal arches. To the right
is an early arch in honour of
Augustus, erected in the
Roman forum in 29 B.C. Below
is a later arch, also in honour
of Augustus, built in the forum
around 20 B.C.

THE POET HORACE

Left: A magistrate wearing a toga edged in
purple. He holds the scroll of the law, which
indicates that he is invested with judicial
authority. In the background is part of the text of
a law carved in bronze.

a poet who wrote with wonderful expression of
personal experiences and daily events, and
Virgil, who wrote Rome's greatest epic, the
Aeneid.

The Development of Imperial Art

The influence of Greek and Hellenistic art
was still seen in Roman art at the time of
Augustus. In his funeral monument, the *Ara
Pacis* in bas-relief, Augustus left a great
testimony to how such older styles influenced
Roman art. All the monuments built to honour
Augustus were based on the idea that artistic
expression must exalt the emperor and the
grandeur of Rome. This tendency was to develop greatly in the first century A.D., when it
was commonly accepted that buildings, sculptures and bas-reliefs should express the idea of
the power and stability of the empire. The
grandeur of Rome also demanded an imposing
scale of public works. In both beauty and
engineering technique, the bridges, aqueducts, city gates, forums and amphitheatres
of the Imperial Age are among the most
impressive achievements of ancient times.

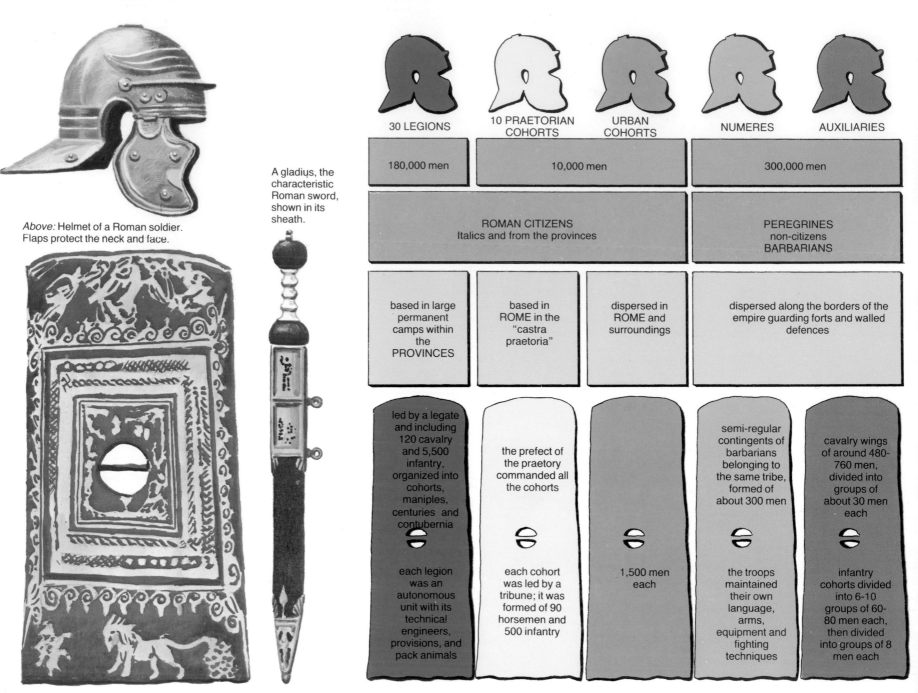

Above: Helmet of a Roman soldier. Flaps protect the neck and face.

A gladius, the characteristic Roman sword, shown in its sheath.

Shield of a legionary.

30 LEGIONS	10 PRAETORIAN COHORTS	URBAN COHORTS	NUMERES	AUXILIARIES
180,000 men	10,000 men		300,000 men	
ROMAN CITIZENS Italics and from the provinces			PEREGRINES non-citizens BARBARIANS	
based in large permanent camps within the PROVINCES	based in ROME in the "castra praetoria"	dispersed in ROME and surroundings	dispersed along the borders of the empire guarding forts and walled defences	
led by a legate and including 120 cavalry and 5,500 infantry, organized into cohorts, maniples, centuries and contubernia	the prefect of the praetory commanded all the cohorts		semi-regular contingents of barbarians belonging to the same tribe, formed of about 300 men	cavalry wings of around 480-760 men, divided into groups of about 30 men each
each legion was an autonomous unit with its technical engineers, provisions, and pack animals	each cohort was led by a tribune; it was formed of 90 horsemen and 500 infantry	1,500 men each	the troops maintained their own language, arms, equipment and fighting techniques	infantry cohorts divided into 6-10 groups of 60-80 men each, then divided into groups of 8 men each

ORGANIZATION OF THE ROMAN ARMY

THE PAX ROMANA

Two Centuries of Peace

The rule of Augustus ushered in a period of exceptional economic, social and political well-being within the Roman Empire. The two centuries of peaceful existence and social development which followed were without parallel in Roman history.

Emperors of the Principate

The imperial model established by Augustus, which resulted in the union of emperor and nobles, army and senate, capital and provinces, gave political tranquillity to the empire throughout the Principate period. Augustus had no heir, but adopted Tiberius, who, after the death of Augustus in A.D. 14, ruled the empire and founded the Julian-Claudian

dynasty. This dynasty ended with the death of Nero in A.D. 68. After a brief period of war between competing Roman armies, Vespasian took power, founding the Flavian dynasty. Upon the death of Domitian in A.D. 96, the senate claimed for itself the right to appoint new emperors. This move allowed the continuation of the fruitful alliance between emperors and the noble class, and put at the head of the Roman empire men who were endowed with high political and moral qualities. These men were not necessarily Roman-born. The Antonine emperors, chosen by the senate, were the most effective in Roman history. Under Trajan and Hadrian the empire reached, by conquest, its maximum extent.

A Cosmopolitan Empire

The Romans felt they had a political and cultural mission to "Romanize" the people of the Mediterranean and Europe. The enterprise of unifying the known civilized world under one rule was successful because Rome did not dominate its subject peoples in an absolute way. Roman rule permitted the coexistence of diverse cultures within the great cosmopolitan empire. But it was remorseless also: those who resisted conquest died in battle or were enslaved.

Participation in Politics

The Romans conceded varying degrees of participation in the political life of the empire to the conquered people. When a group of

A Roman bath

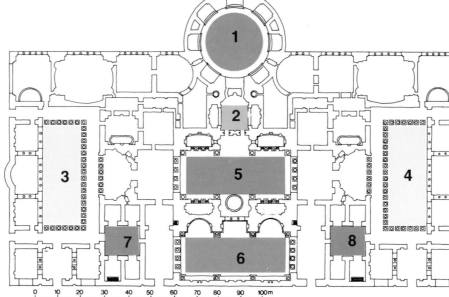

Left: The floor plan of the baths of Caracalla, opened in A.D. 216. An ingenious heating system made it possible to have hot water and rooms maintained at different temperatures throughout the year.

1) Calidarium (Hot bath)
2) Tepidarium (Warm bath)
3-4) Gymnasiums
5) Frigidarium (Cold bath)
6) Swimming pool
7-8) Changing rooms

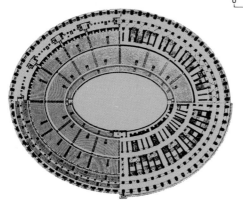

Cross section (*below*) and plan (*above*) of the Flavius amphitheatre, whose construction was started by Vespasian and completed by Titus in A.D. 80. Arenas such as this were used for gladiator fights, animal hunts, and mock naval battles.

The Roman Empire reached its greatest extent in the reign of Trajan (A.D. 98-117).

Below: The remains of the vast amphitheatre at Pompeii. Unlike the Greeks, who built their theatres on hillsides, the Romans built their arenas on flat ground.

Below is a reconstruction of the great circus of Caligula in Rome. It was used for chariot races.

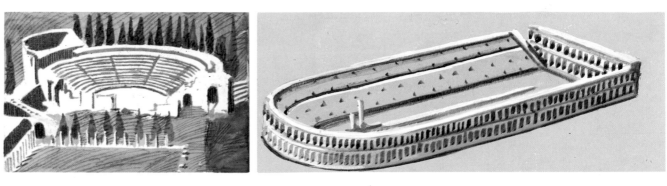

An Empire Built by the Army

Roman citizens settled in a certain site on conquered land, a colony was created giving the inhabitants Roman citizenship with full political rights. When the Romans encountered an existing urbanized society of sufficient sophistication, they allowed it to govern itself to a large extent, as a *civitas*. The inhabitants of the civitas did not have Roman citizenship. If a town was surrounded by a markedly Romanized territory, it would become a *municipium* but its inhabitants would have no right to vote.

Rome's military establishment contributed vastly to the creation of the empire. The army was the main point of contact on the frontier for exchange of customs and Roman values with foreigners.

Roman citizens, immigrants from the provinces, and barbarians from the borders all served in the army under the command of Roman officers. In the Imperial Age, the army was reorganized by Augustus. In his effort to

provide Rome with a permanent and skilled army, Augustus based the military establishment on two pillars – the legions, which were manned by Roman citizens and in the East by Romanized peoples, and the auxilia, military units formed of other conquered peoples of the empire or of barbarians. At the end of the second century A.D., the Roman army numbered about 500,000. The legionary was a professional soldier. On retirement after perhaps 25 years' service, soldiers often settled in colonies near their old bases.

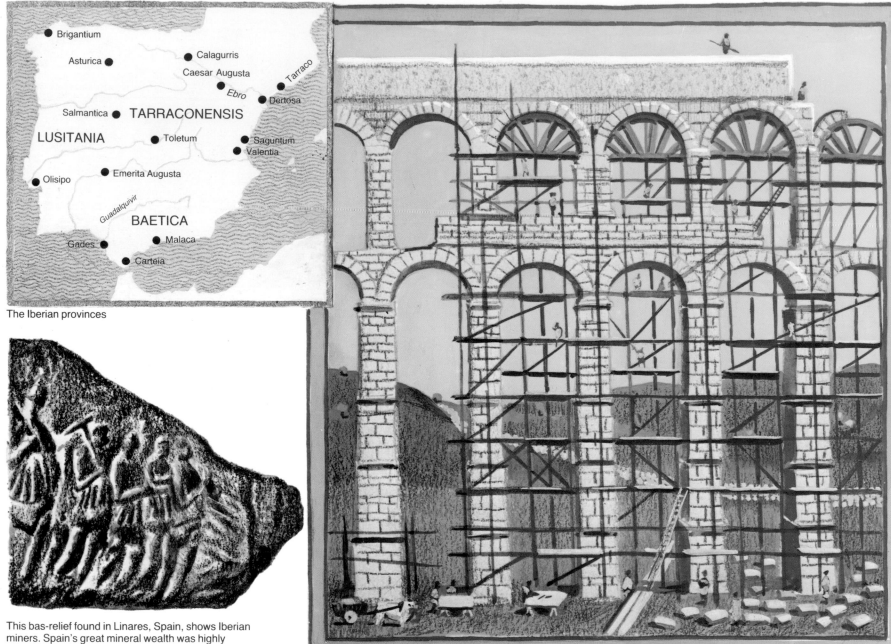

The Iberian provinces

This bas-relief found in Linares, Spain, shows Iberian miners. Spain's great mineral wealth was highly prized by the Romans.

Among the forms of construction in which the Romans excelled were systems for water transportation. Water was a necessity for both farming and urban life. The illustration shows the construction of a two-tier aqueduct across a Spanish valley. The water channel was on the top tier, and the system operated by gravity.

THE PROVINCES OF SPAIN AND GAUL

Spain was the first large Western European region to fall under Roman dominion during the Punic Wars. Prior to the Roman conquest, Iberian, Greek, Carthaginian and Celtic-Iberian peoples lived on the Iberian Peninsula. They were politically organized and grouped in various ways. Some lived in cities and towns, others were tribes of farmers and shepherds. Under Roman administration, Spain was divided into three regions – Baetica, Lusitania and Tarraconensis.

The Economy of the Iberian Provinces

The principal economic riches of Spain came from gold, silver, tin, lead, copper, iron and mercury mines. After the depletion of the Greek mines, Spain had become the main supplier of precious and common metals, which were used throughout the empire. The plentiful production of wheat, oil and wine made a sizeable contribution to the provisions of Rome and Italy as well as Spain. Spain also provided a reserve of infantry and cavalry for the Roman army. The process of Romanization in Spain was especially intensive along the Mediterranean. The northern population put up strong resistance to military conquest, the use of Latin and to the imposition of Roman religion.

Society and Culture

The Roman administration built numerous towns in Spain. At the beginning, they were mainly colonies linked by a vast network of roads. Major aqueduct systems were built with slave labour to ensure the continual supply of fresh water. Aqueducts and dams remain among the most famous Roman monuments to be seen in the region today. Particularly in the first century A.D., Spain contributed greatly to Roman culture. The most important Latin writers of the time were from Spain. Among them were the philosopher Seneca, the poets Lucan and Martial, and the orator and teacher of rhetoric Quintilian. Spain was also the birthplace of two of Rome's most celebrated emperors, Trajan and Hadrian.

The Gauls

Before the Roman conquest, some Greek settlements had been established on the Mediterranean coast of Gaul. The rest of the territory (modern France) was divided among

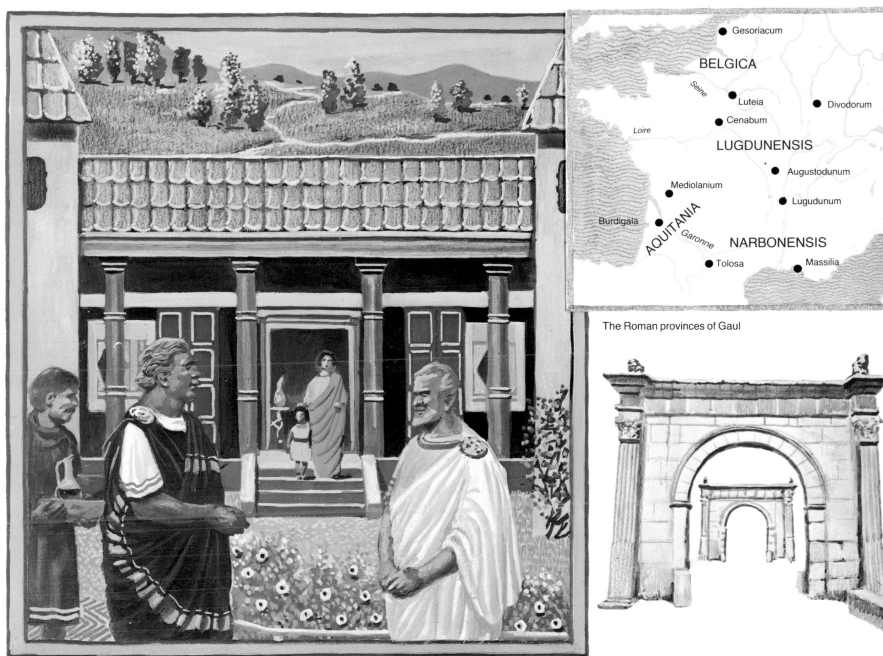

A Gallic-Roman noble welcomes a guest in the yard in front of his villa. The Gauls willingly accepted the Roman way of thinking and behaving.

When the Romans built a provincial town, they often erected a gateway with arches, to commemorate the founding of the town. These are the arches of St. Remy in Provence, France, built at the time of Augustus.

numerous peoples and Celtic tribes. The conquest occurred in several phases. First the southern part of Gaul was taken over, creating the province of Narbonensis Gaul. Later, the central and northern parts were conquered and became the provinces of Aquitania, Lugdunensis Gaul and Belgica Gaul.

Narbonensis Gaul was the province that was Romanized most quickly. The process of Romanization of the other provinces included the construction of towns on the sites of the settlements which had been the former capitals of the different tribes. These towns attained the status of civitas. Each civitas had control over a vast territory, in accordance with the Celtic tradition which maintained a relationship between the tribal centre and the surrounding countryside.

Economic Development

Roman Gaul increased its agricultural resources: wheat, barley, wine, oil, fruit and vegetables. Many of these products were exported, creating problems of competition with other producing nations. The wine of the Gauls, for example, was sold in competition with wine from Italy, traditionally supported by the Roman government. During the course of this "wine battle", the emperors enacted a series of restrictive regulations on vineyards in Gaul.

Artisan activity was widespread in Gaul. Small-scale industries used outside labour, besides the family of the owner. This was the case, for example, in the making of glass and ceramics which replaced, in Western markets, production from Italy.

The Romans used three techniques to build walls (*left to right*)—irregular bricks (opus incertum), diagonally placed bricks (opus reticulatum) and triangular blocks (opus testaceum). Below is a section to show how a Roman road was built. The different layers of materials gave solidity and good water drainage. The surface layer was made of stone slabs that were resistant to wear from traffic. It was cambered, or sloped.

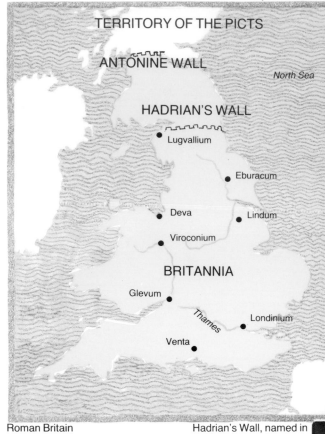

Roman Britain

Hadrian's Wall, named in honour of the emperor was a defensive fortification to keep out the peoples of the northern regions. It was made of stones and turf and followed the contours of the hills. It was furnished with watchtowers and forts, and was regularly patrolled by troops.

This burial stone from the second century A.D. shows a blacksmith pounding an anvil.

The Roman legions came to stay. They built permanent bases, like this one in Germany.

BRITAIN AND THE REGIONS BORDERING THE RHINE

The Conquest of Britain

Britain, or Britannia, at the beginning of its conquest by Rome in 43 B.C., was inhabited by Celts and divided into chiefdoms. These chiefdoms offered strenuous resistance to the Romans for many years. The Romans could never gain control over the whole of the British Isles. Caledonia (Scotland), with its mountainous terrain, always eluded conquest. Hadrian, after A.D. 122, built a fortified wall to guard the frontier. Later emperors pushed the Roman army further north, and a new wall was built in A.D. 140. Beyond this wall was the territory of the unconquered Picts.

Roman Towns in Britain

The majority of the tribal centres in Britain were built on hills and were well protected. According to the Romans, these were not the best sites for a town, which they considered should be the centre of communication for military, commercial and administrative pur-

poses. For this reason, the Romans built their own network of fortresses in locations advantageous for communication. When the period of conquest was over, many of these fortresses were turned into towns. The population grew, and forums and marketplaces were built. Almost all of the British towns attained the status of civitas. Their economic foundations were mainly agricultural. Londinium (London) was an exception to the rule. It grew into an important trading centre, based on its river port and on the network of roads which converged there. It enjoyed great economic prosperity until the end of the second century.

Society and Economy

Only a few Romans settled in the new province, and the majority of the population continued to be Celts. The ruling class was composed of families that were wealthy enough to aspire to senatorial positions, of military officers, and of rich common people.

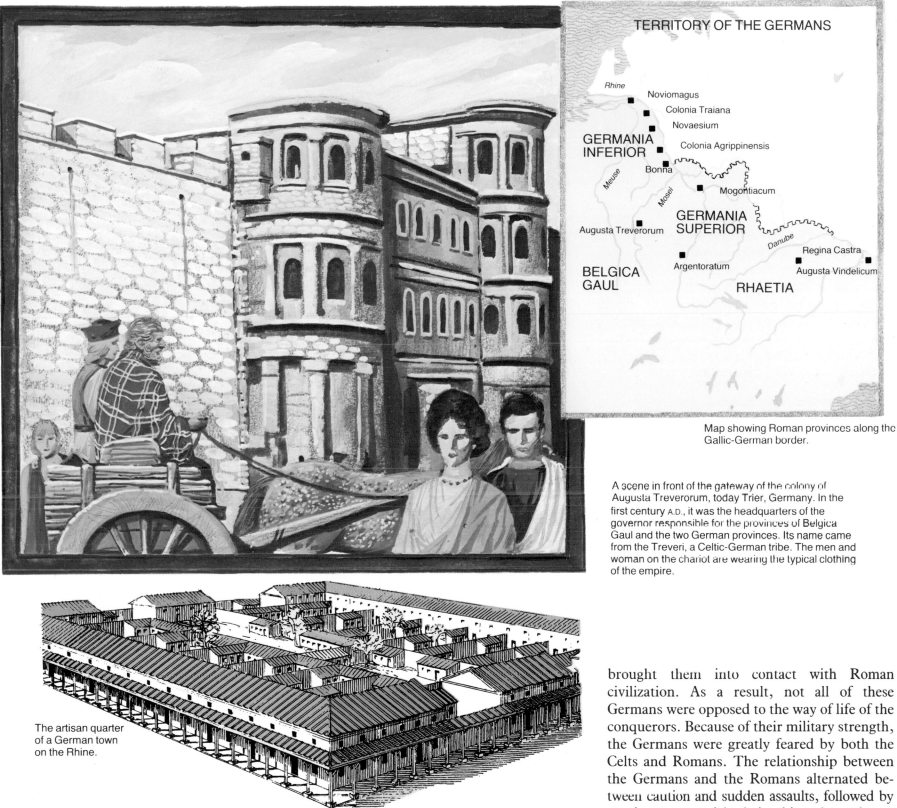

Rhine

Noviomagus

Colonia Traiana

Novaesium

GERMANIA INFERIOR

Colonia Agrippinensis

Bonna

Meuse

Mosel

Mogontiacum

GERMANIA SUPERIOR

Augusta Treverorum

Danube

Regina Castra

BELGICA GAUL

Argentoratum

Augusta Vindelicum

RHAETIA

Map showing Roman provinces along the Gallic-German border.

A scene in front of the gateway of the colony of Augusta Treverorum, today Trier, Germany. In the first century A.D., it was the headquarters of the governor responsible for the provinces of Belgica Gaul and the two German provinces. Its name came from the Treveri, a Celtic-German tribe. The men and woman on the chariot are wearing the typical clothing of the empire.

The artisan quarter of a German town on the Rhine.

These people controlled the governments of the towns. Merchants, artisans and slaves also lived in the towns. Roman customs and behaviour spread among the native Britons, both aristocracy and commoners. The most obvious custom adopted was the wearing of the toga. Latin became the language of government and of culture, while the traditional Celtic language was used in family life. The number of villas rapidly multiplied in the rural areas just outside the towns. The wealth of Roman Britain came from the extraction of coal and metals such as lead, gold and iron.

Rome and the Germans

From the end of the first century B.C., the Germanic population on the Celtic side of the Rhine increased. This was due to the Roman policy of giving tracts of land to farmers, provided they would settle there. This policy caused a great mingling of populations in the regions near the borders. The German tribes had a political organization similar to the Celtic tribes and were much influenced by the Celts living along the Rhine. The custom of serving as auxiliary troops of the Roman army brought them into contact with Roman civilization. As a result, not all of these Germans were opposed to the way of life of the conquerors. Because of their military strength, the Germans were greatly feared by both the Celts and Romans. The relationship between the Germans and the Romans alternated between caution and sudden assaults, followed by treaties, commercial relationships, the exchange of goods and movements of population.

The Romans on the Rhine

The German territories of the Roman empire were divided into Germania Superior and Germania Inferior. They stretched along the Rhine and included lands which are today part of Germany, Holland, Belgium and France. Since this territory lay along the border of the empire, the Romans kept a large military force there, over 100,000 men. The Rhine remained a frontier area, under constant tension.

THE ROMAN EMPIRE AND THE PEOPLES OF THE BALKANS

During the rule of Augustus, the provinces south of the Danube were also conquered by the Romans. These areas were inhabited by various populations. Noricum, Pannonia and the inland areas of the Moesia were inhabited by Celts. Illyrian populations prevailed in the rest of the region.

The Illyrian Lands

The annexation of the Illyrians to the Roman empire opened a new chapter in their history, bringing forth important changes in all areas of material and spiritual life. The Romans further developed the towns which existed along the Adriatic coast. In the countryside and in the rugged mountains, Roman penetration was slower, particularly in the first centuries of Roman domination.

Pannonia

The Romans found the Celts had highly developed agricultural techniques in Pannonia, the vast plain which is today part of Hungary and which stretches all the way to the Danube. The arrival of the Romans caused the development of a wealthy, highly civilized Celtic-Roman world.

The Dacian Wars

The Dacians were a people living along the two banks of the lower reaches of the Danube, between the Black Sea and the Carpathian Mountains. They were descendants of ancient Thracians, but their culture had been influenced by neighbouring steppe peoples. Greece had also influenced the Dacians. These people took on Roman elements, mainly in their economy, defence, and culture. They were an independent people, highly skilled in warfare. They had already made numerous excursions against the Celts of Pannonia and of areas north of the Danube. When the Romans settled along the Danube, Dacian bands frequently raided and looted the Roman provinces.

In A.D. 101, Trajan (who had just been elected emperor) decided to pursue war. The Dacians had learned the fighting techniques of the Romans and had a large army, each soldier armed with a fearsome scimitar. The allies of the Dacians, the Rhoxolani, were nomadic tribes living along the northern coast of the Black Sea. They had armoured cavalry with a full array of weapons. A chain of fortresses surrounded the Dacian capital, Sarmizegetusa. The Romans embarked on the war with great zeal, but the conquest of Dacia required two vigorous campaigns carried out without mercy. The war was finally concluded with the victorious entrance of Trajan into the Dacian capital, the suicide of the Dacian king, and the deportation of the defeated peoples.

The Romanization of the Dacian Lands

In the lands of conquered Dacia, the process of Romanization was carried out mainly through the settlement of Roman people. More and more colonies and municipalities were founded, especially near military camps. The Dacians were reduced in numbers, but not entirely eliminated by war and deportation.

A cavalryman of the Rhoxolani, the allies of the Dacians against the Romans.

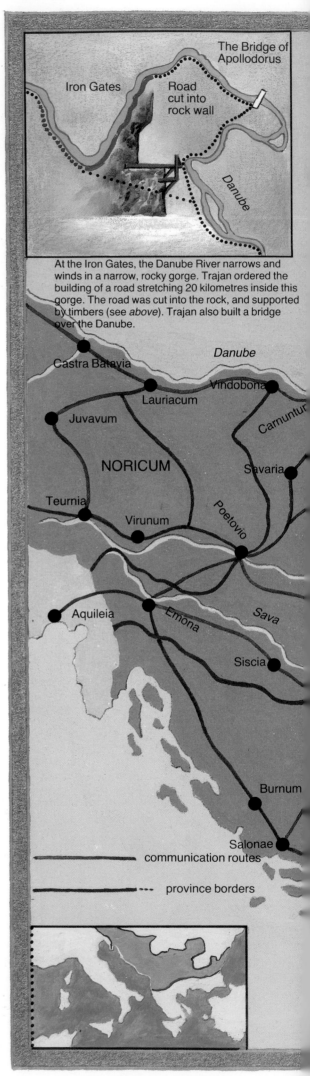

At the Iron Gates, the Danube River narrows and winds in a narrow, rocky gorge. Trajan ordered the building of a road stretching 20 kilometres inside this gorge. The road was cut into the rock, and supported by timbers (see *above*). Trajan also built a bridge over the Danube.

communication routes

province borders

The Balkan-Danube region between the Adriatic and Black seas is shown.

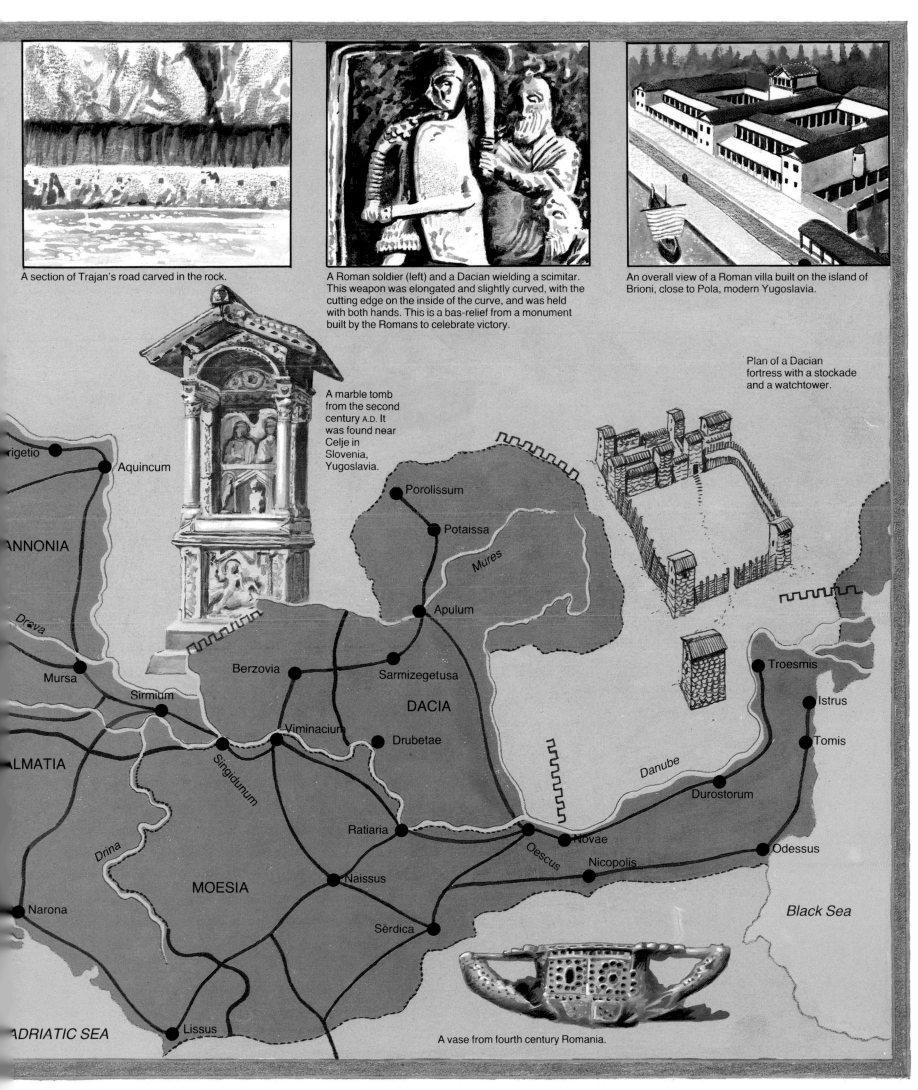

A section of Trajan's road carved in the rock.

A Roman soldier (left) and a Dacian wielding a scimitar. This weapon was elongated and slightly curved, with the cutting edge on the inside of the curve, and was held with both hands. This is a bas-relief from a monument built by the Romans to celebrate victory.

An overall view of a Roman villa built on the island of Brioni, close to Pola, modern Yugoslavia.

A marble tomb from the second century A.D. It was found near Celje in Slovenia, Yugoslavia.

Plan of a Dacian fortress with a stockade and a watchtower.

A vase from fourth century Romania.

Porolissum

Potaissa

Mures

Apulum

ANNONIA

Drava

Mursa

Sirmium

Berzovia

Sarmizegetusa

DACIA

Troesmis

Istrus

LMATIA

Viminacium

Drubetae

Tomis

Singidunum

Danube

Durostorum

Ratiaria

Novae

Odessus

Drina

Oescus

Nicopolis

Naissus

MOESIA

Narona

Black Sea

Serdica

ADRIATIC SEA

Lissus

rigetio

Aquincum

THE EASTERN PROVINCES

Rome and the Hellenistic World

After the death of Alexander the Great, a flourishing civilization of Greek origin, but heavily influenced by Eastern civilizations, developed in the coastal towns of Asia Minor. This was the Hellenistic civilization. The Romans had always feared the commercial expertise of the Greek world and were in deep awe of its cultural superiority. They fought the Greeks and subsequently dominated them, but were also disciples, eager to learn Greek culture and bring it to the West. From the last century of the Republican Age, the Romans brought many works of art and literature to Greece from Rome. With the advent of the Imperial Age, the unity of the Roman world became the main way of spreading Hellenistic culture. The blend of Hellenistic and Roman cultures was productive and allowed the empire to continue ruling the eastern lands for over one thousand years.

Rome's Provinces in Asia Minor and the East

In the Macedonian towns in the regions of Lycia, Pamphylia and Asia Minor, Roman dominion allowed for the enrichment of urban life and favoured the spread of Hellenism to the interior regions. These towns had important strategic locations because they lay on a major trade route between the Mediterranean and the Indian Ocean. Further east, the Cappadocia region and the kingdom of Armenia were geographically isolated from the major commercial routes and centres of culture. However, they slowly absorbed several Hellenistic influences, for the Greek language was spoken at the court of the Armenian king, and many Greeks lived in the country. The Romans conquered Cappadocia first, then Armenia. Armenia was a bulwark against the Parthian kingdom, a powerful enemy of Rome. As a consequence, numerous military posts were established in these regions, and a network of roads was built to move supplies. Moreover, major strategic roads were built to

Shown here: Ephesus, the capital of the Roman province in Asia Minor, reconstructed from evidence found in archaeological excavations. The frieze with ships (top of the page) is a reproduction of a bas-relief found in Ostia, Italy.

Centre map: The provinces of Asia Minor and the Middle East.

connect this land with the Aegean Sea and to facilitate communication with the posts along the Danube. Consequently, the commercial activities in Armenia and Cappadocia greatly increased. Russian wheat, for example, passed through these regions on its way to the military posts along the Euphrates. This borderline with the Parthians represented the furthest reaches of Roman rule in the East.

The Middle East Provinces

Circumstances in the Middle East provinces were in sharp contrast to those in the West. These provinces were Judaea, Syria, Mesopotamia and Assyria. These regions were crossed by major rivers and were rich in fertile plains. They were important commercial centres. Syria in particular, due to its position on the Mediterranean, had always been the starting point of important land communication routes for trade with the Persian Gulf and India.

When the Romans arrived, a flourishing Hellenistic civilization already existed in most of these regions and towns were highly developed. The new Roman provinces were founded on existing administrative regions. Rome sent civil servants only to those areas that already had stable local government. Public works, such as the construction of aqueducts and new irrigation channels, expanded farming into less fertile areas. The production of wheat and other cereals increased. Wine from Syria was imported both by East and West. Olive groves provided plentiful oil, while vast fruit orchards supplied the markets of the empire. Other characteristic Syrian activities were weaving, glassmaking and the production of a rare purple dye, made from sea snails. The camel began to be used for transport, and long camel caravans would leave the city markets of the coast and travel overland, following routes which would pass towns, oases and water wells. The diversity of contacts and the mingling of populations also favoured the spread of different religions. Traditional Greek religion and several Eastern cults coexisted in these Roman provinces. Such exotic mixtures found receptive audiences in the mixed populations of the port and caravan towns, as well as in the army camps.

The marketplace of a town along one of the caravan routes. The Middle East drew its wealth from trade between the Mediterranean and the Orient. The frieze with the camel caravan shown at the top of the page was found in the caravan town of Palmyra.

CHANGES IN ROMAN RELIGION

Religious practices performed by the emperor with great pomp could not meet all the religious needs of a diverse empire. New cults and beliefs arose, often shrouded in mystery.

The Army and the Spread of Mystery Cults

People were looking for answers to their sense of anxiety about life and the uncertainty of the future. Some of this uncertainty was associated with the "nightmare scenario" – the fall of the Roman Empire. An increasing number of people began joining Eastern cults, also called mystery cults. Most of the religious activities of these cults were kept secret from outsiders. Besides the Egyptian cult of Isis, there were the cults of Cybele from Asia Minor, Baal (the warrior god), and Sol Indictus (a sun-god of Syrian origin).

Within the Roman Empire, there were some restrictions about joining cults. The major concern of most Romans was that the cult of the emperor should not be threatened.

The Roman army encountered local cults in the various Eastern provinces where it campaigned. Later, these cults were introduced by the army to Rome and throughout the empire. The new religions seemed to give an answer to the spiritual crises of the people, who in the meantime could continue to take part in the public events of the imperial cult. The faithful could have a personal religious experience which gave them both spiritual peace and a renewed enthusiasm. Processions of the various eastern cults were emotionally moving experiences, very different from the formal rites of Roman religion.

Stoicism

The same sense of discontent over Roman religion was also felt by cultured people, including noble Roman families and even the imperial family. In fact, Roman religion was reduced to public ceremonies and lost any spiritual interest for the people. The way was open for a philosophy called "stoicism" which had started some centuries earlier in Athens through the works of Zeno.

Wisdom was considered to be the ability to recognize the existence of order in the world. People of reason had to accept what happened to them and not give in to emotions. On the one hand, stoicism was pessimistic about the possibilities of changing the circumstances of one's own life or that of other people. On the other hand, it encouraged moderation, a moral effort to lead a virtuous life, humanity, and respect for others. Stoicism gained adherents only among cultured people and the upper class.

An ordinary foot soldier, or legionary, with his equipment. The javelin, or pilum, had an iron head on a wooden shaft. On the march the soldier carried his kit on a pole with a crossbar. Where the Roman army moved, so did the religious beliefs of its soldiers. Beliefs and cults were carried from one end of the empire to the other.

1) Part of a triangular, bronze votive table depicting Baal, the powerful Hittite god of war, being worshipped by soldiers of the empire. He stands on the sacred bull, and above him there is a bust of the sun – Germany, third century A.D. 2) A priest of Cybele is dressed in Oriental fashion holding in his right hand three sprigs of wheat, the symbol of fertility. 3) A procession in honour of Isis.

1   2   3

In the house of a great Roman family, a group of Christians is gathered for a baptism. The new convert will thus become fully part of the Christian community.

CHRISTIANITY

In this uncertain climate, rich in new ideas and spiritual reawakening, came a new event destined to have an impact without precedent in human history. In Palestine, during the reign of Trajan, a man was crucified because he was judged guilty of offending the Hebrew religion. The Roman governor, Pilate, allowed the execution. This man, Jesus of Nazareth, allegedly proclaimed himself son of God, the Messiah of whom the Hebrew scriptures spoke. The writings of the disciples of Jesus, called the Gospels, gave an account of the life and message which Jesus left to humanity. Jesus, also called Christ (or Messiah, which means the consecrated king), brought testimony to the world that God was not an incomprehensible power but was father of all. Christianity was the proclamation of the friendship between God and people. Christ was said to have risen from the dead. For most Hebrews, this was a scandal. They expected a magnificent king, not a common man born in the small village of Bethlehem.

To the Greco-Roman world, Christ seemed a ludicrous figure, a god who had become a man in order to accompany humankind on earth and on to eternity, a god who went as far as being crucified to remove the sins of humanity, a god who told people that if they accepted him he would always be with them. Yet despite ridicule, Christianity survived and the number of people who believed in the new religion grew, slowly but steadily. Christianity spread from Palestine to the rest of the empire, especially in the eastern provinces, in the army, among the common people, and also in the great Roman families. Life as a Christian did not mean the observance of a series of regulations, but it required new, major responsibilities. It called for a new way to perform daily activities because the meaning of life could be found in the smallest detail. Everything could be considered a gesture of love, towards Christ and towards people.

Christians and the Empire

Christians did not deny the sovereignty of the emperor and preached obedience to the law. For this reason, the imperial authorities at first saw no reason to hinder the practice of Christianity. Christians were often helpful in the service of the empire. The imperial administration, however, could not accept the fact that Christians would not worship the emperor as a god. This was considered a break with the Pax Deorum.

The reason for the persecution of Christians was not a fear of political turmoil, but the fear of offending the gods and thereby shaking the solidity of the Roman Empire. Christians were imprisoned, tortured and put to violent death. Even members of the imperial families were sometimes persecuted. Periods of persecution alternated with periods of tolerance. The first persecution was carried out in A.D. 64 by Nero. The second was ordered by Domitian. The rule of the Antonine emperors (especially Hadrian and Antoninus Pius) was a tolerant period during which Christians began to have an influence on Roman culture. But the emperors Decius and Valerian resumed the persecutions. The last major persecution was ordered by Diocletian. Christianity questioned the divinity of the emperor, and in so doing opposed a basic point of the Roman order. On the other hand, it was in agreement with a more important element of Roman civilization—the desire for an alliance with the divine.

THE GERMANS AGAINST THE EMPIRE

A New Aristocracy

At the end of the first century A.D. when the Roman historian Tacitus was writing about Germany, important changes occurred in the part of the German world closest to the empire. These were the result of contact with the Romans, especially with merchants who travelled through German lands. Luxury goods, including riches from the Mediterranean, circulated among the most powerful men of the tribes, and a new wealthy class grew up.

North of the Danube

Since the first century A.D., the tribes of the Marcomanni and Quadi had settled north of the Danube in what is now Czechoslovakia. Being close to the border, they had numerous commercial and cultural contacts with the Roman Empire. They developed an agricultural economy which required more and more land. Gradually, the various tribal groups started to recognize that they had interests and aims in common.

The Roman Frontier Collapses

The Romans living along the Danube were slow to understand and take advantage of the changes that were happening on the other side of the river. The Germans had never been allowed to settle in Roman territory, and they could not cross the Danube. On their side of the river, Romans established a security zone where no barbarians could settle. Around the middle of the second century, barbarians threatened the middle reaches of the Danube. As soon as Rome despatched troops from this border to fight the Parthians, the Germans saw their opportunity. In A.D. 167, the Marcomanni, Quadi and twenty other German tribes under King Bellovesus attacked across stretches of the Danube. The Roman troops were weakened by a serious outbreak of plague, and did not resist. The Germans, after devastating Pannonia, reached Italy. They arrived in Venetum and laid siege to Aquileia.

The Romans Counter-Attack

It was a difficult time for Rome. Many soldiers and officers were dead, and the empire had inadequate financial resources. The emperor Marcus Aurelius assumed personal leadership of the army. The Germans were forced to abandon Italy in A.D. 172, and the Roman legions counter-attacked.

Right: In A.D. 170, German tribes made the first raid on Italy, breaking through from the Tarvisio or from the Slovenian Alps.

The incursions of Marcomanni and Quadi across the Danube into the empire.

The Plan of Marcus Aurelius

Marcus Aurelius hoped victory would allow the further expansion of the empire. He planned to create two provinces beyond the Danube, Marcomannia and Sarmatia. The new border was to be in the northern mountains, which were easy to defend. However, Marcus Aurelius died in Vienna in A.D. 180 and was succeeded by his son, Commodus, who did not carry out his father's plan.

Right: During the last phase of the war, the Roman army crossed the Danube and for a short time established a base north of the river.

Two iron spear points used by the Germans, with magical signs engraved in silver.

Above are Roman soldiers with prisoners and cattle, the spoils of war. This image is from the Column of Antoninus.

Diocletian ordered that a great palace be built for him in Spalatum on the Yugoslavian coast. The palace was composed of several buildings surrounded by a fortified enclosure. In building his palace, Diocletian blended architectural styles and details from throughout the empire.

THE EMPIRE IN CRISIS AND DIOCLETIAN'S RULE

The Third Century, A Period of Crisis

The death of Commodus in A.D.192 opened a dramatic period in Roman history. The Romans lived with fears concerning the future, and a sense of the imminent fall of the empire was in the air. The ancient Etruscan prophecies about the rise and fall of civilizations in history seemed on the verge of coming true for Rome. Famine and pestilence caused a major crisis in some provinces, such as Britain. Robberies by an undisciplined army and barbarian raids weakened the countryside, affecting even wealthy people. Villas were abandoned and all agricultural activities stopped. The economic crisis was followed by a monetary crisis, mostly due to the great expense of maintaining the army. Taxes were heavy, yet never sufficient. The emperors started minting copper coins instead of silver ones, and the currency soon devalued, causing steep price increases.

The Emperors Septimius Severus and Caracalla

In A.D. 193, troops from the provinces marched on Rome, led by the African Lucius Septimius Severus. He was the commander of the Pannonian army and became emperor after defeating three rivals. Upon his death, his son Caracalla ascended the throne. In A.D. 212, Caracalla issued a constitution which granted Roman citizenship to all the free inhabitants of the empire. This completed a process of Romanization which had lasted for centuries but was also a sign that the Roman Empire was changing. All the citizens were equal. But they were now ruled by a despotic sovereign, more like an Eastern king than the earlier Roman rulers.

Pressure from the Barbarians

Taking advantage of Rome's internal turmoil, barbarian tribes broke through the border at several points and swarmed into the empire. German tribes formed an alliance and made plans to conquer the European provinces. Franks and Alemanni threatened Gaul, Saxons raided Britain and Gaul, and Marcomanni attacked along the Danube.

The Army Elects the Emperors

The death of Severus Alexander in A.D. 235 was followed by anarchy. The empire fell under the control of the army. Between A.D. 235 and A.D. 285, twenty-six emperors elected by various military factions alternated in ruling the empire. No strong authority existed, trade suffered, and the provinces were in ruins.

Inserts (at top of page) show aspects of Rome's crisis in the third century A.D. From left to right: Political instability and the frequent assassination of the emperors; pressure from the barbarians; looting and devastation carried out by rebellious troops; and the desertion of country villas, which were no longer safe places to live.

Diocletian and the Tetrarchy

Several general-emperors tried to restore order. In A.D. 284, the army proclaimed the Illyrian general Valerius Aurelius Diocletian emperor. The people were tired of riots and assassinations. They longed for peace and were willing to collaborate in a reform policy. Diocletian introduced the system of tetrarchy (a government of four people).

He divided the territory of the empire. Each half was ruled by two men – a senior "Augustus", who was the ruler, and a "Caesar" who was his heir. Diocletian ruled the eastern provinces from Nicomedia in Asia Minor. His Caesar lived in the Balkans. The Augustus of the western provinces was Maximian, who lived in Milan. His Caesar lived in Trier. The tetrarchy was also meant to solve the problem of imperial succession because each Caesar was eventually to become Augustus without previous approval by the senate or acclamation by the legions. Diocletian himself started the succession process, abdicating in A.D. 305 and retiring to his palace in Spalatum on the Dalmatian coast.

The Administrative System and the Reform of the Army

The power of the emperor remained absolute, and his will was enforced by a tight network of officials. This system caused the collapse of the ancient nobility and of the traditional Roman magistratures. The imperial administration ruled with military discipline, and as a result the unity of the empire was strengthened. Huge masses of soldiers were drafted to live among the less Romanized populations. The army numbered as many as 350,000 soldiers. In the face of massive recruitment, the old provincial armies lost much of their importance. They were composed of colonists who had a hereditary duty to serve in the army. Great fortifications were built to protect the main towns and cities of the empire.

The Persecution of Christians

In order to sustain his power, Diocletian proclaimed himself to be the ruler sent by Jupiter and affirmed that his power had a divine origin. Therefore, he revived the practice of the imperial cult. In A.D. 303, he launched the last violent and major persecution against the Christians, who had become numerous throughout the empire and had made converts among the military and civilians.

Soldiers arrest a Christian.

Right: In Italy in A.D. 311, Constantine fought for leadership of the empire against the other Augustus, Maxentius. The two armies clashed in Rome, on the Tiber, close to the Milvian Bridge. On top of a temporary pontoon bridge, the troops of Maxentius were defeated by those of Constantine, who had put a Christian symbol on their shields.

Constantine is acclaimed Augustus by his troops in York, in A.D. 306.

Left: Rome was full of magnificent buildings as this reconstruction of its forum in the Imperial Age shows. Constantine renewed and completed the basilica which Maxentius had started.

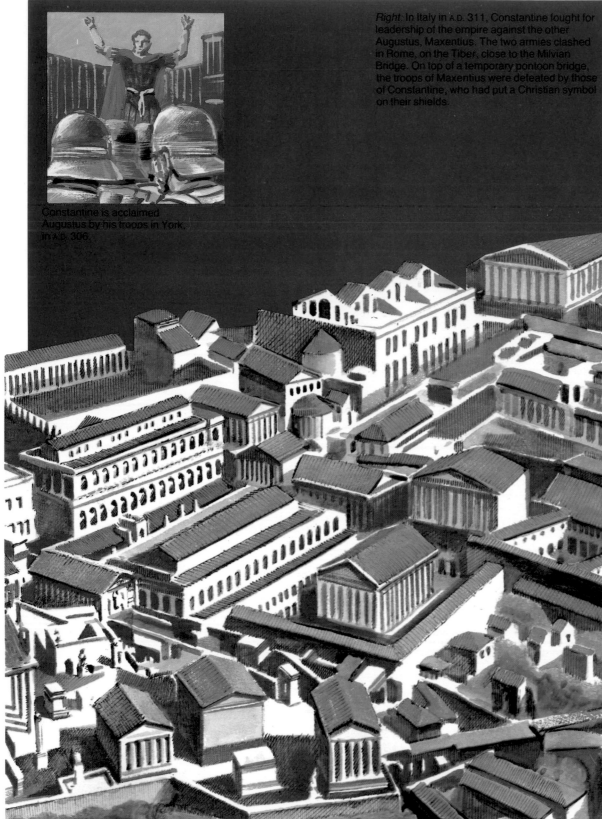

to display a symbol of Christianity on their shields. Trying to escape, Maxentius was drowned. In A.D. 324, Constantine defeated his last rival, Licinius, in the eastern provinces and became sole ruler of the empire.

Constantine and Christianity

Christianity had survived Diocletian's persecution, and both the distribution and the strength of the new faith became increasingly evident. The Church was becoming a major force, exerting a lasting influence on society. In A.D. 313 in Milan, Constantine issued an edict in which he conceded freedom of worship for all religions. He was the first Christian emperor.

The Second Rome

The eastern provinces now became the most important part of the empire. The economy, based on sea trade and overland caravan routes, was flourishing. The borders which most needed to be patrolled were in the East and in the Balkans. Thus, the centre of the empire needed to move eastwards, for both economic and strategic reasons. Another reason prompted Constantine to abandon Rome. The city symbolized Rome's pagan past, while the eastern provinces were becoming the most vital centres of Christianity.

Constantine decided to build a new city on the Bosphorus Strait, where the sea lanes of the Aegean Sea and the Black Sea met. The new city, capital of the empire, was Byzantium, later called Constantinople, and now Istanbul. It was meant to rival Rome in grandeur and in the abundance of public buildings and monuments, but it would not

FROM ROME TO BYZANTIUM

The Failure of the Tetrarchy

The solution to the problem of central authority devised by Diocletian did not last long. After abdicating, Diocletian helplessly witnessed internal struggles between Augustuses and Caesars for the division of power. After several years of confused struggle, Constantine, another Illyrian general, finally triumphed.

The Rise of Constantine

Constantine was proclaimed Augustus by his legions in York, in A.D. 306. In A.D. 311, he entered Rome and fought for power against his rival Maxentius, the other Augustus who had been elected in Rome. The following year, he finally defeated Maxentius in the battle of the Milvian Bridge. Constantine had had a vision of a cross in the sky, and ordered his soldiers

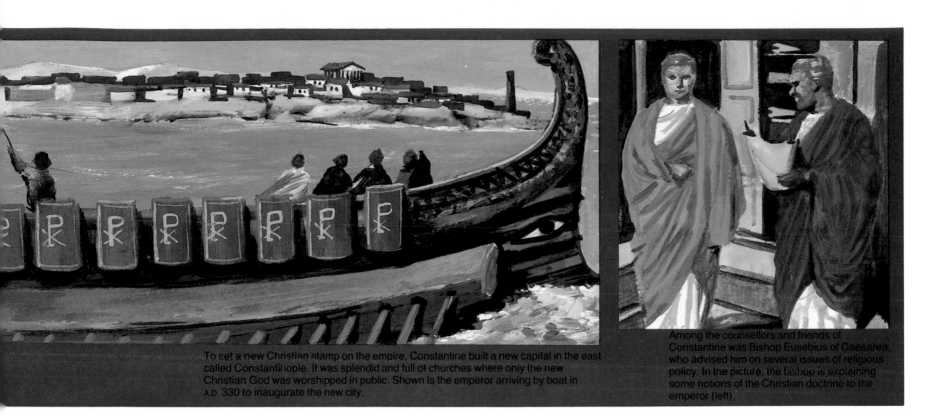

To set a new Christian stamp on the empire, Constantine built a new capital in the east called Constantinople. It was splendid and full of churches where only the new Christian God was worshipped in public. Shown is the emperor arriving by boat in A.D. 330 to inaugurate the new city.

Among the counsellors and friends of Constantine was Bishop Eusebius of Caesarea, who advised him on several issues of religious policy. In the picture, the bishop is explaining some notions of the Christian doctrine to the emperor (left).

have public sites for pagan cults. It was to be a Christian city. The city plan was carefully drawn, and construction proceeded rapidly. Works of art from all of the Hellenistic Orient were collected in the city, and the best craft workers were employed. On May 11, in A.D. 330, Constantine solemnly inaugurated the new city, the second Rome.

The Christian Roman Empire

The transformation which had begun over fifty years earlier was complete. The Roman Empire of Augustus no longer existed. The emperors enjoyed greater status, divine in person and judgement, as Rome's real power declined. A solemn ritual, derived from Persian rites, was used as people paid elaborate homage to the imperial majesty. The emperor had unlimited authority. A huge number of officials carried out his will, even in the most remote towns of the empire.

The Decline of Rome

Rome and its empire were in increasing danger. War and invasions by its foes threatened the centuries-old Roman order. Rome was doomed to disintegrate but it had richly endowed civilizations yet to come. Byzantium was the city which preserved the tradition of Rome at its best, while Christianity gave a new meaning to human life and destiny. From Byzantium, the most important features of classical Roman civilization were to be passed on to Europe. The last years of Roman imperial rule marked the end of the ancient world. A new chapter was opening in the history of the Western world.

A Roman archer serving in a unit of auxiliary troops from the eastern provinces.

Caledonia

Antonine Wall

Hadrian's Wall

York

BRITANNIA

London

ATLANTIC OCEAN

Rhine

GERMANIA

Colonia

Mainz

Treviri

Paris

Strasbourg

Danube

RAETIA

Vienna

Budapest

Alesia

NORICUM

Sarmizegetusa

GAUL

Celje

Aquileia

DACIA

Bordeaux

Milan

PANNONIA

Pola

Sirmium

Zara

Danube

DALMATIA

Aix

Spalatum

Nis

MOESIA

Marseilles

ITALY

THRAC

Numantia

MACEDONIA

HISPANIA

Rome

Saguntum

Gades

Ath

ACHAIA

Tangier

Syracuse

Sparta

Agrigentum

Cirta

Carthage

MAURETANIA

AFRICA PROCONSOLARIA

Mediterranean Sea

Cyrene

Sabrata

Leptis Magna

CYRENAICA

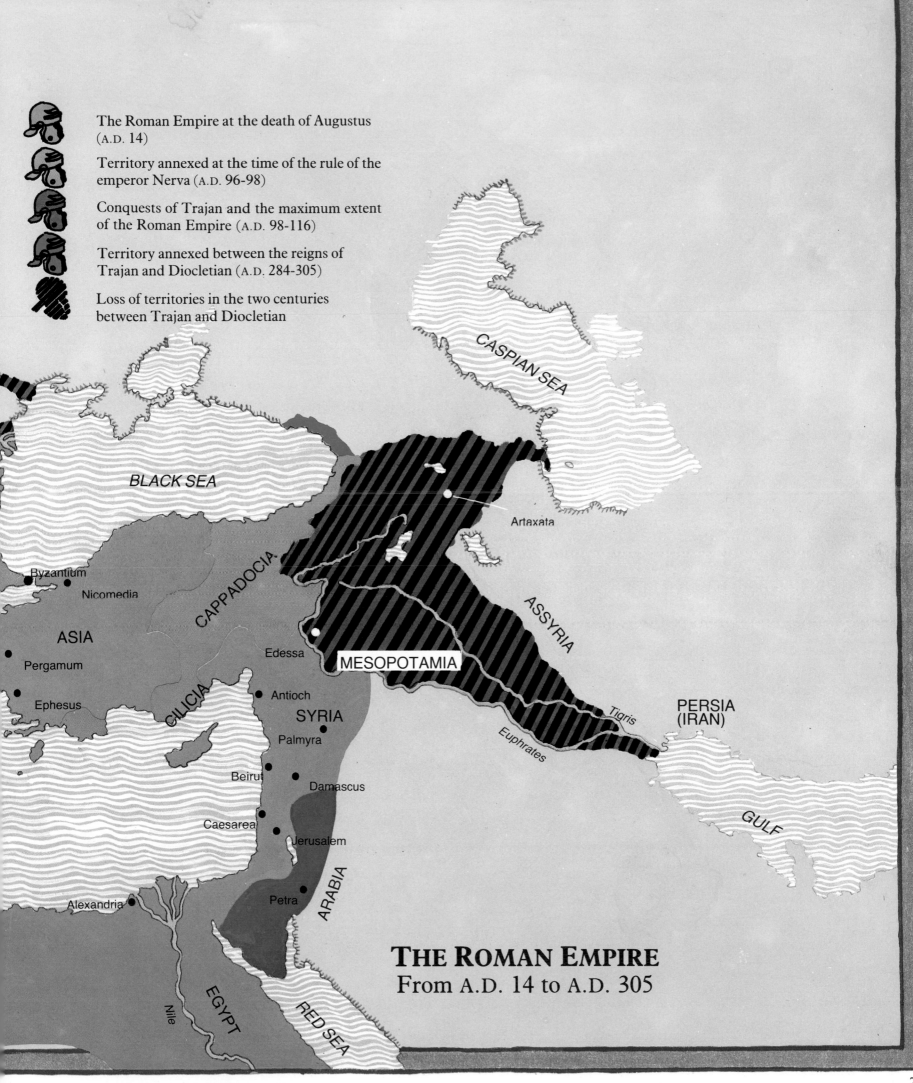

The Roman Empire at the death of Augustus (A.D. 14)

Territory annexed at the time of the rule of the emperor Nerva (A.D. 96-98)

Conquests of Trajan and the maximum extent of the Roman Empire (A.D. 98-116)

Territory annexed between the reigns of Trajan and Diocletian (A.D. 284-305)

Loss of territories in the two centuries between Trajan and Diocletian

CASPIAN SEA

BLACK SEA

Artaxata

Byzantium

Nicomedia

CAPPADOCIA

ASSYRIA

ASIA

Pergamum

Edessa

MESOPOTAMIA

PERSIA (IRAN)

Ephesus

CILICIA

Antioch

SYRIA

Tigris

Palmyra

Euphrates

Beirut

Damascus

GULF

Caesarea

Jerusalem

ARABIA

Alexandria

Petra

THE ROMAN EMPIRE
From A.D. 14 to A.D. 305

Nile

EGYPT

RED SEA

71

GLOSSARY

aggressive: ready and willing to fight or take action; eager to participate fully.

agora: a meeting place or assembly area.

agriculture: the processes and activities associated with farming; the work of planting seeds, producing crops and raising animals.

aqueduct: a pipe system used to transport water from a distant place.

archaic: of or belonging to ancient times.

artisan: a skilled craft worker.

autonomous: capable of existing alone and apart from others.

barbarian: originally a person who was not Greek or could not speak Greek. Later it came to mean anyone who was not Roman and who belonged, in the Roman view, to a primitive or uncivilized tribe or group.

ceramics: objects made of clay that are moulded into shape and baked in an oven.

cuirass: a leather breastplate, used as armour by the ancient Greek warriors.

cult: a specific or distinct type of religious worship or ritual. Greek religion is usually identified with the cult of the gods of Mount Olympus.

cultivate: to prepare land for the planting and growing of crops.

culture: the traditions, skills, habits and systems of different groups of people at different times in history.

currency: the medium of exchange, or money used, in any country or region.

deity: a god; a being who possesses a divine nature.

demiurge: a magistrate or other person given the power to administer the law.

democracy: a government which is in the hands of the people.

dialogue: a conversation between two or more people. Plato used dialogue as a method of teaching and learning.

dynasty: a family of rulers; the period of time during which a specific family is in power.

environment: the circumstances or conditions of a plant or animal's surroundings. The physical and social conditions of an organism's environment influence its growth and development.

expedition: a journey or exploratory mission undertaken in order to achieve a specific purpose.

frieze: a series of decorations positioned to form a border around a room or building.

gladiator: a man who fought with weapons against other men or animals in an arena in Ancient Rome. Gladiators fought as a form of entertainment for the public.

heritage: cultural characteristics that are passed on from one generation to the next.

ingot: a piece of metal, formed into the shape of a bar, used as currency in ancient times.

javelin: a spearlike weapon.

lottery: a game based on luck or chance, in which people buy numbered tickets in the hope of winning prizes or money.

magistrate: a government official who is granted the powers to dispense justice.

maritime: having to do with the sea or with the shipping industry.

melancholy: the condition of being sad, gloomy, or depressed.

mercenary: hired soldier; soldier paid to fight battles in foreign countries.

migrate: to move from place to place in search of food and shelter. Migration usually revolves around seasonal changes.

minority: a small portion of an otherwise large group; less than half of the whole.

mint: to make money or other currency which is authorized by the government.

monarch: the primary ruler of a state or kingdom, such as a king or queen.

monologue: a long speech delivered by one person. Ancient Greek actors often delivered monologues.

oligarchy: a government run by a few select people. Noblemen formed oligarchies in Ancient Greece.

oracle: any person who is believed to be capable of communication with the gods.

orator: a person who is skilled at delivering speeches in public. The Greek Pericles was an excellent orator.

patrician: in the society of Ancient Rome, a member of a noble or prominent family. Most political positions of that time were held by patricians.

peninsula: a land area almost entirely surrounded by water and connected to the mainland by a narrow strip of land called an isthmus.

pessimism: the attitude toward life that the worst will always happen; the belief that more bad than good exists in the world.

plebeian: in the society of Ancient Rome, one of the common people or the lower classes.

polis: a city-state in Ancient Greece. Politics is a word of Greek origin meaning involvement in the business of the polis.

prehistoric: referring to a period of time before recorded history.

primitive: of or existing in the beginning or the earliest times; ancient.

produce: crops grown by farmers, such as wheat, fruit and vegetables.

prologue: an introduction; the first part or portion of a literary work used as preparation for what follows.

revenue: income; the money which a business or government is able to generate for itself through taxation, profit and other sources.

ritual: a system of acts or procedures, especially with regard to religious worship.

sanctuary: a place of peace or safety; a haven or place of rest; a special building set aside for holy worship.

siren: in Greek mythology, one of several beautiful women who lured sailors to their deaths along rocky coastlines. The sailors could not resist the haunting songs of the sirens.

sovereign: a supreme ruler; one who possesses authority above all others.

tragedy: a type of play invented by the Greeks that deals with unhappy events.

tyrant: a supreme ruler, usually one who disregards the wishes or opinions of his subjects.

valley: a stretch of low land that lies between hills or mountains and usually has a stream or river flowing through it.

vineyard: an area of land used to grow grapes, usually for the purpose of making wine.

INDEX